Basics of Coin Grading for U.S. Coins

by Ken Bressett

Fully illustrated, easy-to-use guide.
Contains Official Grading Standards established
by the American Numismatic Association

D1558144

WHITMAN COIN PRODUCTS
RACINE, WISCONSIN 53404

356   ISBN: 0-307-93562-0   Printed in U.S.A.

INTRODUCTION

Grade, the condition or state of wear of a coin, is one of the main factors affecting a coin's value. Until the last few decades, grading was done by "instinct." Based on knowledge and personal observations, one seller would have one system, and another seller with varying observations, experiences, and opinions, would have a different system - there was little standardization.

Since the 1950's coin values have increased sharply. In many instances, coins that were worth $10 twenty years ago, are worth $200 or more now. A very small difference in grade can mean a very large difference in price. The exact grade of a coin is more important today than ever before.

This book has been designed to enable the average reader to successfully grade coins as easily and simply as possible by following a proven system that gives accurate results. Terms and standards used throughout the text are based on accepted practices of experienced dealers and collectors.

A more detailed analysis of systematic coin grading is fully presented in *Official A.N.A. Grading Standards for United States Coins,* and is the basis for this condensed handy version. While not intended to be a substitute for the comprehensive A.N.A. text, this book covers the essential elements for grading frequently encountered coins.

WEAR

When a coin first begins to show signs of handling or abrasion (wear), only the highest parts of the design are affected. Evidence that such a coin has been circulated can be seen by carefully examining the high spots for changes in color, surface texture, or sharpness of fine details.

In early stages of wear, the highest points of design become slightly rounded or flattened, and the very fine details begin to merge together. After a coin has been in circulation for a short time, the entire design and surface will show light wear. Many of the high parts will lose their sharpness, and most of the original luster will begin to wear away (except in recessed areas). Continued circulation will reduce the sharpness and relief of the entire design, causing high points to merge with the next lowest part of the design. When the protective rim is worn away, the entire surface becomes flat, and most of the details blend together or become partially merged with the surface.

LIGHTING AND MAGNIFICATION

The same coin can have a different appearance depending upon the lighting conditions and also the amount of magnification used to examine it. We recommend that a magnifying glass of four to eight power be used. This is sufficient to reveal all the differences and peculiarities necessary to grade the coin accurately. Under extreme magnification (10 power or more), even the finest coin may show many exaggerated marks and imperfections making grade interpretation difficult.

Recommended illumination for grading is a 100 watt incandescent light bulb located approximately three feet from the coin. Incandescent light provides a pinpoint light source and enables surface characteristics to be studied in more detail. Flourescent light, which spreads illumination from a diffused origin, is apt to conceal minute differences.

Hold the coin between your fingertips over a soft surface (to prevent damage in the event of dropping) and at an angle, so that light reflects from the coin's surface into your eye. Turn or rotate the coin horizontally so that different characteristics can be observed in better detail. You should also examine the edge for blemishes (which will be discussed later in this text).

UNCIRCULATED COINS

The term "Uncirculated," interchangeable with "Mint State," refers to a coin which has never experienced circulation. Such a piece has no wear of any kind. A coin as bright as the time it was minted or with barely visible (light) natural toning can be described as "Brilliant Uncirculated." An Uncirculated coin which has more noticeable (light to moderate) natural toning can be described as "Toned Uncirculated." The presence or absence of light toning does not usually affect an Uncirculated coin's grade. In fact, a premium is often paid for silver coins which are characterized by attractive, natural toning. However, black or very dark (heavy) natural toning that blankets the entire surface of an Uncirculated coin can result in lowering its value.

The quality of sheen or "mint luster" on an Uncirculated coin is an essential element, and has a bearing on its desirability. Luster may in time become dull, frosty, spotted or discolored. Unattractive luster will normally lower the value.

With the exception of certain Special Mint Sets made in recent years for collectors, Uncirculated or normal production strike coins were produced on high speed presses, stored in bags together with other coins, run through counting machines, and in other ways handled without regard to numismatic posterity. As a result, it is the rule and not the exception for an Uncirculated coin to have bag marks and evidence of coin-to-coin contact, even though the piece might not have seen actual commercial circulation. Generally speaking, the value of an Uncirculated coin is affected by the number of bag marks that are present.

CIRCULATED COINS

Once a coin enters circulation it begins to show signs of wear. As time goes on, the coin becomes more worn until, after a period of many decades, only a few features may be left.

The following definitions of circulated grades are intended only as a general outline. Because wear often occurs in different spots on different designs, refer to specific information about various types in the text which follows this introduction.

About Uncirculated. Only a small trace of wear is visible on the highest points of the coin. Considerable mint luster is still present.

Extremely Fine. Light overall wear on the coin's highest points. All design details are very sharp. Mint luster is usually seen only in protected areas of the coin's surface, such as between the star points and in the letter spaces.

[4]

Very Fine. Light even wear on the entire surface design. Details on the highest points lightly worn, but with all lettering and major features sharp.

Fine. Moderate to considerable even wear. Entire design is bold. All lettering, including the word LIBERTY (on coins with this feature on the shield or headband) visible, but with some weaknesses.

Very Good. Well worn. Most fine details such as hair strands and leaf details are worn nearly smooth. The word LIBERTY, if on a shield or headband, is only partially visible.

Good. Heavily worn. Major designs visible, but with faintness in areas. Head of Liberty, wreath, and other major features visible in outline form, but without center detail.

About Good. Very heavily worn with portions of the lettering, date, and legends being worn smooth. The date barely readable.

MAJOR CHARACTERISTICS OF A COIN'S SURFACE

Bag Marks. The term "bag mark" refers to a nick, small cut, or other similar mark on a coin's surface. These marks occur during the minting process and also when the coins come into contact with each other in mint bags while being stored in the Treasury Department, or in bank vaults. It is usual for nearly all Uncirculated coins to have some bag or contact marks. In time, the effects of circulation may wear away all evidence of any bag marks.

The larger and heavier a coin, the more bag marks it may have. Older coins were often affected by peculiarities of the striking mint. For example, double eagles struck at Carson City, Nevada (a remote location), nearly always have very heavy bag marks. This is attributable to the rigors of transportation from the Carson City Mint and also to the somewhat primitive conditions (when compared with Philadelphia) which existed at the time.

Scratches. Scratches are grooves or marks on a coin's surface which result from careless handling. Scratches, if prominently visible, merit consideration because they detract from the value of a coin.

Edge Bumps (Nicks or Dents). A coin, particularly a heavy one, dropped inadvertently, and impacting with a hard surface against its rim, will usually acquire an edge bump. Like other surface injuries, edge bumps reduce the value of a coin to some extent, depending more or less upon severity.

Die Weakness. Die weakness originates from several causes. After extensive use, certain design features on a die tend to become worn, resulting in weak areas on the struck coins. Often when a die became too worn it was reground and replaced with a new one or in some instances re-engraved, then pressed back into service.

Another cause of weak-appearing coins occurred when some areas of the die were weak to begin with. At times, portions of the central design were only lightly impressed into the die, thus causing a weakness in the coin design, usually on the areas in lower relief. Further, improperly hardened dies had a tendency to sink in certain areas, which transmitted as a weakness to the coin.

Striking Weakness. Most weaknesses on modern coins are a result of striking. Striking weakness takes many different forms. Several times throughout United States coinage history, a design was prepared which left directly opposing areas of high relief on the obverse and reverse dies. When this occurred striking pressure was often inadequate, or not enough metal was available in the blank coinage disk (planchet) to be pushed up fully into the recesses of both dies. The result was a weakness in the design on the coin.

CLEANING COINS

In a word - "don't" (unless it's absolutely crucial to the preservation of the coin)! Over time, coins naturally acquire layers of oxides, most of which actually protect their surfaces. When cleaning solutions such as coin "dips" and abrasive compounds are used in an attempt to renew the appearance of a coin, this protection is stripped away leaving the surface exposed to other (and perhaps more aggressive) forms of oxide buildup.

Most beginning collectors have the idea that cleaning a coin will improve it. For every coin in some way improved by cleaning, it is fair to say that a dozen or more have been decreased in value. Generally, experienced collectors agree that a coin should not be cleaned unless there are spots of corrosion (pitting which might worsen in time) or unsightly streaking or discoloration.

GLOSSARY

The following list contains frequently used coin-collecting terms which, when used in a hobby context, differ from their everyday use.

Abrasions - Light rubbing or scuffing from friction (not the same as hairlines or bag marks).

Adjustment Marks - Small striations or file marks found on early United States coins. Caused during planchet preparation (before striking) by drawing a file across the blanks to remore excess metal so as to reduce the planchet to its proper weight. The result is a series of parallel grooves.

Bag Mark - A surface mark, usually in the form of a nick, acquired by a coin when making contact with others in a mint bag. Bag marks are more common on large, heavy, silver and gold coins than on smaller pieces.

Blemishes - Minor nicks, marks, flaws or spots of discoloration that mar the surface of a coin.

Business Strike - A coin intended for circulation in the channels of commerce (as opposed to a Proof coin specifically struck for collectors).

Clash Marks - Impressions of the reverse design on the obverse of a coin, or vice-versa. This can result when a planchet fails to enter the impact area and the striking dies collide with each other, causing features of the design to transfer from one die to the other.

Die Defect - An imperfection in a coin caused by a defective die.

Die Variety - A variation of a design attributed to a particular die. For example, over a dozen different dies were used, all hand cut, to manufacture large cents during one year. In one way or another, each die had its own unique characteristics which were imparted to the coins it produced.

Field - That portion of the coin's surface not used for a design or inscription.

First Strike - An unofficial term referring to a coin struck shortly after the new die is put into use. Such coins often have Prooflike surfaces and resemble Proofs in certain (but not all) characteristics. (Resurfaced dies sometimes have these characteristics.)

Hairlines - A series of minute lines or scratches, usually visible in the field of a coin, caused by cleaning or polishing.

High Points - Areas of highest relief in a coin design. The first small parts to show evidence of wear or abrasion.

Incuse - See Relief.

Legend - The principal inscription on a coin.

Lettered Edge - The narrow edge of a coin bearing an inscription. Found on some foreign and older United States coins.

Lintmarks - Small incuse or incised marks on the surface of a Proof or Uncirculated coin caused by stray hairs, threads, and the like adhering to the die after it was wiped with an oily rag.

Luster - The glossy mint sheen on the surface of an Uncirculated coin. Although normally brilliant, in time luster may become dull, frosty, spotted or discolored.

Matte Proof - A special type of Proof finish used at the Philadelphia Mint prior to World War I. This method was first employed by the Paris Mint and was later adopted for a limited time during the 1908-1916 years for certain (but not all) issues by the Philadelphia Mint. The surface is prepared by a special pickling process which gives it a grainy appearance.

Micro - Very small or microscopic.

Milled Edge - A raised rim around the outer surface of a coin. Not to be confused with the reeded or serrated narrow edge of the coin.

Mint Error - A misstruck or defective coin produced by a mint.

Mint Luster - The "sheen" on the surface of a Mint State or nearly Mint State coin. Caused by a layer of microscopic crystals formed during the striking process.

Mint Mark - A symbol, usually a small letter, used to indicate at which mint a coin was struck.

Nick - A small mark on a coin caused by another coin bumping against it or by contact with a rough or sharp object.

Obverse - The front or face side of a coin, generally the side with the date and the principal design.

Oxidation - The formation of oxides or tarnish on the surface of a coin from exposure to air, dampness, industrial fumes, or other elements.

Planchet - The blank piece of metal on which a coin design is stamped.

Processing - A term describing the mistreatment of a coin by wire brushing, acid dipping, or otherwise abrading or eroding the surface in an effort to make it appear in a higher grade than it actually is.

Proof - Coins struck for collectors using specially polished or otherwise prepared dies. Most Proof coins can be distinguished by a highly reflective, mirrored surface (except Matte Proofs).

Prooflike - Describes an Uncirculated coin with partial proof surface, but lacking the full characteristics of a Proof.

Reeded Edge - The edge of a coin with grooved lines that run vertically around its perimeter. (The edge found on all current United States dime, quarter, half and dollar coins.)

Relief - Any part of a coin's design that is raised above the coin's surface is said to be in relief. The opposite of relief is *incuse*.

Reverse - The side of a coin carrying the design of lesser importance. Opposite of the obverse side.

Rim - The raised portion of a coin encircling the obverse and reverse which protects the designs of the coin from wear.

Scratch - A deep line or groove in a coin caused by contact with a sharp or rough object.

Striations - Thin, light raised lines on the surface of a coin, caused by excessive polishing of the die.

Striking - Refers to the process by which a coin is minted. Also refers to the sharpness or design details. A sharp strike or strong strike is one with all of the details struck very sharply; a weak strike has the details lightly impressed at the time of coining.

Toning - Oxide layers formed on a coin's surface. Caused usually by long-term exposure to gases in the atmosphere (originating naturally or from man-made sources, or both). The discoloration resulting from toning is often very attractive, and many collectors prefer coins with this feature.

Weak Strike - A coin with certain of its details not fully formed because of the hardness of alloy, insufficient striking pressure, or improper die spacing.

Whizzing - The harsh treatment of a coin by wire brushing, acid dipping, or otherwise removing metal from the coin's surface to give it the artificial appearance of being in a higher grade. Whizzing is an alteration (not a grade or condition) and reduces the value of the coin.

GRADING ABBREVIATIONS

Following are grade names with corresponding abbreviations commonly used by collectors and dealers to describe the *basic* condition of their coins:

Typical Uncirculated: Unc.
About Uncirculated: Abt. Unc. or AU
Extremely Fine: Ex. Fine or EF
Very Fine: V. Fine or VF
Fine: F
Very Good: V. Good or VG
Good: G
About Good: Abt. Good or AG

Note: It is important to point out that additional grading distinctions which include numerical designations, have evolved from several of the basic grades given above, but which go beyond the scope and purpose of this introductory text. This concise book is intended to help readers acquire essential skills toward development of a thorough knowledge for grading all United States coins. For readers who become active collectors we highly recommend the comprehensive **Official A.N.A. Grading Standards for United States Coins,** *by the American Numismatic Association.*

HOW TO USE THIS BOOK

The coin grades described in this book are intended for use in determining the relative condition of coins in various states of preservation. Coins are listed in order of ascending denomination from half cents to gold pieces. Within each denomination, design types are listed in chronological order. Match your coins with the illustrations and brief italic descriptions, then read the adjacent text. If a coin does not quite fit the text description, then try the next higher or next lower grade.

It should be emphasized that because of variables in the minting process, some coins may be found which do not conform exactly with the standard definitions of wear as given in this text.

HALF CENTS—1800–1808
UNCIRCULATED
Absolutely no trace of wear.

A coin exactly as it was minted, with no trace of wear or injury. May lack full mint luster; color is usually an even light brown.

Check points for signs of abrasion: hair at forehead; ear; edge of ribbon on wreath; leaves above and beside HALF.

ABOUT UNCIRCULATED
Small trace of wear visible on highest points.

OBVERSE: Traces of wear show on hair at forehead, the ear, and on the highest point of the shoulder.

REVERSE: Leaves, bow knot and ribbon show slight wear on the edges and ribs.

Surface is still somewhat lustrous.

EXTREMELY FINE
Very light wear on only the highest points.

OBVERSE: Wear extends on hair from forehead to left of ear, at back of head, and along the high ridge near the shoulder.

REVERSE: Slight wear evidence on most of the leaves and high points of bow and ribbon.

HALF CENTS—1800–1808
VERY FINE
Light to moderate even wear. All major features are sharp.

OBVERSE: Parts of hair worn from top of head to drapery but some details show. Balance of hair left of eye distinct. Folds in drapery show wear.

REVERSE: Leaves are worn flat and show very few details. Bow is well worn but bold.

FINE
Moderate to heavy even wear. Entire design clear and bold.

OBVERSE: Hair worn from top of head to drapery, but will still show some detail. Hair above forehead worn almost smooth. Legend and date worn but clear. Some details remain in drapery.

REVERSE: Leaves and bow heavily worn but edges still show. Leaves below CENT still have some visible details. Legend is worn but clear.

VERY GOOD
Well worn. Design clear but flat and lacking details.

OBVERSE: Only the hair ends show detail. Shoulder and drapery worn smooth. The eye shows clearly. Legend and date are readable.

REVERSE: Only the outline of leaves and bow show. Legend is complete but some letters may be weak.

HALF CENTS—1800–1808

GOOD
Heavily worn. Design and legend visible but faint in spots.

OBVERSE: The hair shows no detail. Parts of eye show, but drapery and shoulder are worn smooth. Legend weak but readable.

REVERSE: Leaves complete but well worn. Bow knot and ribbon well outlined. Tops of some letters worn flat.

ABOUT GOOD
Outlined design. Parts of date and legend worn smooth.

OBVERSE: Head is outlined with all details worn away. Legend and date very weak but mostly visible.

REVERSE: Entire design is partially worn away. Only half of the letters in legend are readable.

HALF CENTS—1809–1836

UNCIRCULATED
Absolutely no trace of wear.

A coin exactly as it was minted, with no trace of wear or injury. May lack full mint luster; color is usually an even light brown.

Check points for signs of abrasion: hair adjacent to LIBERTY; edge of ribbon and bow; leaves above H and LF in HALF.

ABOUT UNCIRCULATED
Small trace of wear visible on highest points.

OBVERSE: There are traces of wear in hair adjacent to LIBERTY, and on the highest point above the shoulder.

REVERSE: Slight wear shows on bow and edges of leaves near H and LF. Surface is still somewhat lustrous.

EXTREMELY FINE
Very light wear on only the highest points.

OBVERSE: Wear shows above LIBER and to the right of eye below those letters. Some wear shows on curls at back of head.

REVERSE: Slight wear on most of of the leaves and high parts of ribs above H, bow and ribbon ends.

HALF CENTS—1809–1836

VERY FINE
Light to moderate even wear. All major features are sharp.

OBVERSE: Parts of hair worn from top of head to shoulder, but some details show. Balance of hair and ribbon distinct. Curls on shoulder are quite flat. LIBERTY is clear. Star details are weak.

REVERSE: Leaves are worn flat and show very few details. Bow is well worn.

FINE
Moderate to heavy even wear. Entire design clear and bold.

OBVERSE: Hair worn from top of head to bottom of neck, but will still show some detail. Hair ribbon and LIBERTY worn but readable. Stars have no central detail.

REVERSE: Leaves and bow heavily worn, but edges will show some detail. Legend is worn but clear.

VERY GOOD
Well worn. Design clear but flat and lacking details.

OBVERSE: Hair ends and parts near eye show some detail. LIBERTY is readable. The eye and ear are visible. Rim, stars and date are clear.

REVERSE: Only the outline of leaves and bow show. Legend is complete, but some letters may be very weak.

HALF CENTS—1809–1836

GOOD
Heavily worn. Design and legend visible but faint in spots.

OBVERSE: Hair shows no detail. Parts of LIBERTY show, but ear, eye and rim are worn smooth. Stars weak but visible.

REVERSE: Half of letters in the legend are visible. Wreath is worn smooth with bow and ribbon outlined.

ABOUT GOOD
Outlined design. Parts of date and legend worn smooth.

OBVERSE: Head is outlined with all details worn away. Date very weak but readable. LIBERTY and stars only partially visible.

REVERSE: Entire design and rim is partially worn away. Only a few letters in the legend are readable.

HALF CENTS—1840-1857
UNCIRCULATED
Absolutely no trace of wear.

A coin exactly as it was minted, with no trace of wear or injury. May lack full mint luster; color is usually an even light brown.

Check points for signs of abrasion: hair above ear; bow of ribbon on wreath; leaves beside HALF.

ABOUT UNCIRCULATED
Small trace of wear visible on highest points.

OBVERSE: Traces of wear near ear, and on high points of curls on neck and below bust.

REVERSE: Leaves beside H and F show slight wear on the edges and ribs. There is a trace of wear on bow.

Surface is still somewhat lustrous.

EXTREMELY FINE
Very light wear on only the highest points.

OBVERSE: Wear above and to right of ear, at tip of coronet, and along the high curls on the shoulder.

REVERSE: Slight wear shows on most of the leaves and high parts of bow.

HALF CENTS—1840–1857

VERY FINE
Light to moderate even wear. All major features are sharp.

OBVERSE: Parts of hair worn from top of head to upper neck, but some details show. Balance of hair and coronet distinct. Shoulder curls are quite flat.

REVERSE: Leaves are worn flat and show only partial details. Part of bow is well worn.

FINE
Moderate to heavy even wear. Entire design clear and bold.

OBVERSE: Hair worn from top of head to bottom of neck, but will still show some detail. Coronet shows wear along upper edge. Beads on hair cord sharp and LIBERTY bold. Stars and date worn but sharp.

REVERSE: Leaves and bow heavily worn, but edges and a few details still show. Legend is worn but bold.

VERY GOOD
Well worn. Design clear but flat and lacking details.

OBVERSE: Hair shows detail only in spots, mostly around the bun. The coronet is outlined and hair cord shows clearly. LIBERTY is worn but complete.

REVERSE: Only a bold outline of the leaves and bow show. Legend is complete but some letters may be weak.

GOOD
Heavily worn. Design and legend visible but faint in spots.

OBVERSE: Hair and bun show very few details. Parts of LIBERTY, the coronet, and the eye show. Hair cord still has some visible beads.

REVERSE: Most letters in the legend are visible.

ABOUT GOOD
Outlined design. Parts of date and legend worn smooth.

OBVERSE: Head is outlined with nearly all details worn away. Stars and date very weak but visible.

REVERSE: Entire design is partially worn away. Only half of letters in the legend are readable.

LARGE CENTS—DRAPED BUST 1796–1807

UNCIRCULATED
Absolutely no trace of wear.

A coin exactly as it was minted, with no trace of wear or injury. May lack full mint luster; color is usually an even light brown.

Check points for signs of abrasion: high points of hair at forehead and above the ear; high points of leaves adjacent to S and second T in STATES.

ABOUT UNCIRCULATED
Small trace of wear visible on highest points.

OBVERSE: Traces of wear show at forehead and on the highest points of drapery.

REVERSE: Leaves below S and second T in STATES show slight wear on edges and high spots.

Surface is still somewhat lustrous. Minor blemishes detract from quality of surface.

EXTREMELY FINE
Very light wear on only the highest points.

OBVERSE: Slight wear extends from forehead to ear. Drapery is worn in spots but clearly defined.

REVERSE: Slight wear on most of the leaves. Three-quarters of ribbing shows.

Minor blemishes detract from surface quality.

LARGE CENTS—DRAPED BUST 1796–1807

VERY FINE
Light to moderate even wear. All major features are sharp.

OBVERSE: Parts of hair worn from top of head to upper ear, but some details show. Balance of hair distinct. Bust and drapery at shoulder are quite flat

REVERSE: One-third of the ribbing in leaves can be seen. Bow and knot worn but bold.

FINE
Moderate to heavy even wear. Entire design clear and bold.

OBVERSE: Hair worn from top of head to bottom of neck, but still shows two-thirds of details. Parts of drapery folds are visible.

REVERSE: Leaves and bow well worn, but some ribbing still shows. Legend is worn but very clear.

VERY GOOD
Well worn. Design clear but flat and lacking details.

OBVERSE: Only the back third of hair ends show detail. Drapery is worn nearly smooth. Parts of eye and curl on neck show. Legend and date are readable.

REVERSE: Only the outline of leaves and bow show. Legend is complete, but some letters may be weak.

LARGE CENTS—DRAPED BUST 1796–1807

GOOD
Heavily worn. Design and legend visible but faint in spots.

OBVERSE: Hair and ribbon show no detail. Drapery at shoulder is worn smooth. Legend weak but readable.

REVERSE: Letters in legend are barely visible. Ribbon ends merge with surface.

ABOUT GOOD
Outlined design. Parts of date and legend worn smooth.

OBVERSE: Head is outlined with all details worn away. Legend and date partially worn away but visible.

REVERSE: Entire wreath is faint but visible. Only a few letters in the legend are readable.

LARGE CENTS—CLASSIC HEAD 1808-1814

UNCIRCULATED
Absolutely no trace of wear.

A coin exactly as it was minted, with no trace of wear or injury. May lac[k] full mint luster; color is usually an even light brown.

Check points for signs of abrasion: high points of hair at forehead an[d] above the eye; high points of leaves adjacent to O and T in denomination[.]

ABOUT UNCIRCULATED
Small trace of wear visible on highest points.

OBVERSE: Traces of wear show at forehead and above the eye.

REVERSE: Leaves and ribbon show slight wear on the high spots.

Surface is still somewhat lustrous. Minor blemishes detract from quality o[f] surface.

EXTREMELY FINE
Very light wear on only the highest points.

OBVERSE: Slight wear extends from forehead to below LI. The curls near th[e] ear are worn but clearly defined.

REVERSE: Slight wear on bow and most of the leaves. Three-quarters o[f] ribbing shows in leaves.

Minor blemishes detract from surface quality.

LARGE CENTS—CLASSIC HEAD 1808–1814

VERY FINE
Light to moderate even wear. All major features are sharp.

OBVERSE: Parts of hair worn from top of head to shoulder, but all major details show. Star details are weak.

REVERSE: Leaves are worn but one-third of ribbing shows. Bow is well worn.

FINE
Moderate to heavy even wear. Entire design clear and bold.

OBVERSE: Hair worn from top of head to bottom of neck, but will still show about two-thirds detail. Stars have no central detail.

REVERSE: Bow and leaves heavily worn, but edges still show some ribbing. Legend is worn but clear.

VERY GOOD
Well worn. Design clear but flat and lacking details.

OBVERSE: Hair ends and curls are smooth but show some detail. LIBERTY is readable. The eye and ear are visible. Stars and date are clear.

REVERSE: Only the outline of the leaves and bow show. Legend is complete, but some letters may be very weak.

GOOD
Heavily worn. Design and legend visible but faint in spots.

OBVERSE: Hair shows no detail. LIBERTY is readable, but ear, eye and rim are worn smooth. Stars weak but visible.

REVERSE: Letters in legend are well worn but visible. Wreath is worn smooth with bow and ribbon outlined.

ABOUT GOOD
Outlined design. Parts of date and legend worn smooth.

OBVERSE: Head is outlined with all details worn away. Date very weak but readable. LIBERTY and stars only partially visible.

REVERSE: Entire design and rim are partially worn away. Only a few of the letters in the legend are readable.

LARGE CENTS—CORONET 1816–1839

UNCIRCULATED
Absolutely no trace of wear.

A coin exactly as it was minted, with no trace of wear or injury. May lack full mint luster; color is usually an even light brown.

Check points for signs of abrasion: hair adjacent to LIBERTY; edge of ribbon and bow; leaves above O and E in ONE.

ABOUT UNCIRCULATED
Small trace of wear visible on highest points.

OBVERSE: Traces of wear evident in hair above the eye, and on the curl in front of the ear.

REVERSE: Leaves near O and E in ONE, and the bow, show slight wear on the edges.

Surface is still somewhat lustrous.

EXTREMELY FINE
Very light wear on only the highest points.

OBVERSE: Wear shows above LIBER and to the right of eye below those letters. Some wear shows on curls at back of head and in front of the ear. Hair cords are sharp.

REVERSE: Slight wear shows on most of the lettering, high parts of leaves, and the bow and ribbon ends.

LARGE CENTS—CORONET 1816–1839

VERY FINE

Light to moderate even wear. All major features are sharp.

OBVERSE: High parts of hair worn but show three-quarters detail. Balance of hair and cords are distinct. Curls on shoulder and star details are weak.

REVERSE: Leaves are worn and show only half of details. Bow and lettering are well worn but sharp.

FINE

Moderate to heavy even wear. Entire design clear and bold.

OBVERSE: Hair worn from top of head to bottom of neck, but will still show most of detail. Hair cords and LIBERTY worn but bold. Stars have no central detail.

REVERSE: Leaves and bow heavily worn, but some ribbing still shows. Legend is worn but clear.

VERY GOOD

Well worn. Design clear but flat and lacking details.

OBVERSE: About half of the hair detail is visible. Back hair cord and half of inner cord show clearly. The eye and ear are visible. Rim, stars and date are clear.

REVERSE: Only the outline of bow and parts of the leaf stems show. Legend is complete, but some letters may be weak.

LARGE CENTS—CORONET 1816–1839

GOOD
Heavily worn. Design and legend visible but faint in spots.

OBVERSE: Hair shows no detail. Parts of LIBERTY and about half of back hair cord show, but ear, eye and rim are worn nearly smooth. Stars weak but visible.

REVERSE: All letters in legend are visible but very weak. Wreath is worn smooth with bow and ribbon outlined.

ABOUT GOOD
Outlined design. Parts of date and legend worn smooth.

OBVERSE: Head is outlined with all details worn away. Date very weak but readable. LIBERTY and stars only partially visible. Stars partially worn away.

REVERSE: Entire design and rim is partially worn away. Most letters in the legend are readable.

LARGE CENTS—BRAIDED HAIR 1840–1857
UNCIRCULATED
Absolutely no trace of wear.

A coin exactly as it was minted, with no trace of wear or injury. May lack full mint luster; color is usually an even light brown with traces of red.

Check points for signs of abrasion: hair above ear; bow of ribbon on wreath; high points of leaves.

ABOUT UNCIRCULATED
Small trace of wear visible on highest points.

OBVERSE: There are traces of wear near ear, and on high points of curls or neck and below bust.

REVERSE: High points of leaves show slight wear on the edges and ribs.
There is a trace of wear on bow.
Surface is still somewhat lustrous.

EXTREMELY FINE
Very light wear on only the highest points.

OBVERSE: Wear visible at top of head, above eye, to right of ear, at tip of coronet, and along the high curls on the shoulder.

REVERSE: Slight wear shows on most of the leaves and high parts of the bow

LARGE CENTS—BRAIDED HAIR 1840–1857

VERY FINE
Light to moderate even wear. All major features are sharp.

OBVERSE: Parts of hair worn from top of head to upper neck, but most details are sharp. Balance of hair and coronet distinct. Shoulder curls are flattened.

REVERSE: Leaves are worn at high points and show only half of the details. Bow is well worn.

FINE
Moderate to heavy even wear. Entire design clear and bold.

OBVERSE: Hair worn from top of head to bottom of neck, but still will show some detail. Coronet shows wear along upper edge. Beads on hair cord and LIBERTY bold. Stars and date worn but sharp.

REVERSE: Leaves and bow heavily worn, but edges and some details still show. Legend is worn but bold.

VERY GOOD
Well worn. Design clear but flat and lacking details.

OBVERSE: Hair shows detail only in spots, mostly around the bun. The coronet is outlined and the hair cord shows clearly. LIBERTY is worn but complete.

REVERSE: Only a bold outline of the leaves, stems and bow show. Legend is complete, but some letters may be weak.

LARGE CENTS—BRAIDED HAIR 1840-1857

GOOD
Heavily worn. Design and legend visible but faint in spots.

OBVERSE: Hair and bun show very few details. Parts of LIBERTY, the coronet, and the eye show. Hair cord still has some visible beads.

REVERSE: Most of the letters in legend are visible.

ABOUT GOOD
Outlined design. Parts of date and legend worn smooth.

OBVERSE: Head is outlined with nearly all details worn away. Stars and date very weak but visible.

REVERSE: Entire design is partially worn away. Only half of the letters in legend are readable.

SMALL CENTS—FLYING EAGLE 1856–1858

UNCIRCULATED
Absolutely no trace of wear.

A coin exactly as it was minted, with no trace of wear or injury. Must have full mint luster and brilliance or light toning. Any unusual die or planchet traits must be described.

ABOUT UNCIRCULATED
Small trace of wear visible on highest points.

OBVERSE: Traces of wear show on the breast, left wing tip, and head.
REVERSE: Traces of wear show on the leaves and bow.
  Half of the mint luster is still present.

EXTREMELY FINE
Very light wear on only the highest points.

OBVERSE: Feathers in wings and tail are plain. Wear shows on breast, wing tips, head and thigh.
REVERSE: High points of the leaves and bow are worn.

SMALL CENTS—FLYING EAGLE 1856–1858

VERY FINE
Light to moderate even wear. All major features are sharp.

OBVERSE: Breast shows considerable flatness. Over half of the details are visible in feathers of the wings. Head worn but bold. Thigh smooth, but feathers in tail are complete.

REVERSE: Ends of leaves and bow worn smooth.

FINE
Moderate to heavy even wear. Entire design clear and bold.

OBVERSE: Some details show at breast, head, and tail. Outlines of feathers in right wing and tail show with no ends missing.

REVERSE: Some details visible in the wreath. Bow is very smooth.

VERY GOOD
Well worn. Design clear but flat and lacking details.

OBVERSE: Outline of feathers in right wing ends show but some are smooth. Legend and date are visible. The eye shows clearly.

REVERSE: Slight detail in wreath shows, but the top is worn smooth. Very little outline showing in the bow.

SMALL CENTS—FLYING EAGLE 1856–1858

GOOD
Heavily worn. Design and legend visible but faint in spots.

OBVERSE: Entire design well worn with very little detail remaining. Legend and date are weak but visible.

REVERSE: Wreath is worn flat but completely outlined. Bow merges with wreath.

ABOUT GOOD
Outlined design. Parts of date and legend worn smooth.

OBVERSE: Eagle is outlined with all details worn away. Legend and date readable but very weak and merging into rim.

REVERSE: Entire design partially worn away. Bow is merged with the wreath.

SMALL CENTS—INDIAN HEAD 1859–1909

UNCIRCULATED
Absolutely no trace of wear.

A coin exactly as it was minted, with no trace of wear or injury. Must have full mint luster and brilliance or light toning. Any unusual die or planchet traits must be described.

ABOUT UNCIRCULATED
Small trace of wear visible on highest points.

OBVERSE: Traces of wear show on the hair above ear and curl to right of ribbon.

REVERSE: Traces of wear show on the leaves and bow knot.
Half of the mint luster is still present.

EXTREMELY FINE
Very light wear on only the highest points.

OBVERSE: Feathers well defined and LIBERTY is bold. Wear shows on hair above ear, curl to right of ribbon and on the ribbon end. Most of the diamond design shows plainly.

REVERSE: High points of the leaves and bow are worn.

[34]

SMALL CENTS—INDIAN HEAD 1859–1909

VERY FINE
Light to moderate even wear. All major features are sharp.

OBVERSE: Headdress shows considerable flatness. Nearly half of the details still show in hair and on ribbon. Head slightly worn but bold. LIBERTY is worn but all letters are complete.

REVERSE: Leaves and bow are almost fully detailed.

FINE
Moderate to heavy even wear. Entire design clear and bold.

OBVERSE: One-quarter of details show in the hair. Ribbon is worn smooth. LIBERTY shows clearly with no letters missing.

REVERSE: Some details visible in the wreath and bow. Tops of leaves are worn smooth.

VERY GOOD
Well worn. Design clear but flat and lacking details.

OBVERSE: Outline of feather ends show but some are smooth. Legend and date are visible. At least three letters in LIBERTY show clearly, but any combination of two full letters and parts of two others are sufficient.

REVERSE: Slight detail in wreath shows, but the top is worn smooth. Very little outline showing in the bow.

SMALL CENTS—INDIAN HEAD 1859–1909

GOOD
Heavily worn. Design and legend visible but faint in spots.

OBVERSE: Entire design well worn with very little detail remaining. Legend and date are weak but visible.

REVERSE: Wreath is worn flat but completely outlined. Bow merges with wreath.

ABOUT GOOD
Outlined design. Parts of date and legend worn smooth.

OBVERSE: Head is outlined with nearly all details worn away. Legend and date readable but very weak and merging into rim.

REVERSE: Entire design partially worn away. Bow is merged with the wreath.

SMALL CENTS—LINCOLN 1909 TO DATE

UNCIRCULATED
Absolutely no trace of wear.

A coin exactly as it was minted, with no trace of wear or injury. May lack full mint luster, and surface may be dull or spotted.

Check points for signs of abrasion: high points of cheek and jaw; tips of wheat stalks.

ABOUT UNCIRCULATED
Small trace of wear visible on highest points.

OBVERSE: Traces of wear show on the cheek and jaw.

REVERSE: Traces of wear show on the wheat stalks.
   Three-quarters of the mint luster is still present.

EXTREMELY FINE
Very light wear on only the highest points.

OBVERSE: Wear shows on hair above ear, on the cheek, and on the jaw.

REVERSE: High points of wheat stalks are worn, but each line is clearly defined.
   Traces of mint luster still show.

SMALL CENTS—LINCOLN 1909 TO DATE

VERY FINE
Light to moderate even wear. All major features are sharp.

OBVERSE: Head shows considerable flatness. Nearly all the details still show in hair and on the face. Ear and bow tie worn but bold.

REVERSE: Lines in wheat stalks are worn but plain and without weak spots.

FINE
Moderate to heavy even wear. Entire design clear and bold.

OBVERSE: Some details show in the hair. Cheek and jaw are worn nearly smooth. LIBERTY shows clearly with no letters missing. The ear and bow tie are visible.

REVERSE: Most details are visible in the stalks. Top wheat lines are worn but separated.

VERY GOOD
Well worn. Design clear but flat and lacking details.

OBVERSE: Outline of hair shows but most details are smooth. Cheek and jaw are smooth. More than half of bow tie is visible. Legend and date are clear.

REVERSE: Wheat shows some details and about half of the lines at the top.

SMALL CENTS—LINCOLN 1909 TO DATE
GOOD
Heavily worn. Design and legend visible but faint in spots.

OBVERSE: Entire design well worn with very little detail remaining. Legend and date are weak but visible.

REVERSE: Wheat is worn nearly flat but is completely outlined. Some grains are visible.

ABOUT GOOD
Outlined design. Parts of date and legend worn smooth.

OBVERSE: Head is outlined with nearly all details worn away. Legend and date readable but very weak and merging into rim.

REVERSE: Entire design partially worn away. Parts of wheat and motto merged with the wreath.

Note:

The Memorial cents from 1959 to date can be graded by using the obverse descriptions.

TWO CENTS—1864–1873

UNCIRCULATED
Absolutely no trace of wear.

A coin exactly as it was minted, with no trace of wear or injury. Must have full mint luster and brilliance or light toning. Any unusual die or planchet traits must be described.

ABOUT UNCIRCULATED
Small trace of wear visible on highest points.

OBVERSE: Traces of wear show on the word WE and at tips of the leaves.

REVERSE: Traces of wear show on leaves and ribbons.
    Half of the mint luster is still present.

EXTREMELY FINE
Very light wear on only the highest points.

OBVERSE: WE worn but well defined and bold. Slight wear shows on horizontal lines of the shield. High points of leaves and arrows are worn but show all details.

REVERSE: Leaves and wheat are worn but all details are visible.

TWO CENTS—1864–1873

VERY FINE
Light to moderate even wear. All major features are sharp.

OBVERSE: WE shows considerable flatness, but all letters in motto are clear. Over half the details still show in leaves. Shield worn but bold.

REVERSE: Leaves and ribbon are worn. Wheat grains are all visible.

FINE
Moderate to heavy even wear. Entire design clear and bold.

OBVERSE: Some details show in leaves and shield lines. Entire motto is plain but WE is very weak.

REVERSE: Some details visible in the wreath. Bow is very smooth but ribbons are distinct.

VERY GOOD
Well worn. Design clear but flat and lacking details.

OBVERSE: Outline of leaves and arrows show but parts are smooth. Motto is weak and WE is incomplete. Only a few vertical shield lines show separations.

REVERSE: Slight detail in wreath shows, but the knot is still clear. Very little outline showing in bow.

TWO CENTS—1864–1873

GOOD
Heavily worn. Design and legend visible but faint in spots.

OBVERSE: Entire design well worn with very little detail remaining. IN GOD and TRUST are very weak but visible.

REVERSE: Wreath is worn nearly flat but is completely outlined. Legend is weak but readable.

ABOUT GOOD
Outlined design. Parts of date and legend worn smooth.

OBVERSE: Design is outlined with nearly all details worn away. Date readable but very weak and merging into rim.

REVERSE: Entire design partially worn away. Bow is merged with wreath. Only parts of the legend are visible.

THREE CENTS—SILVER 1851–1873

The first three-cent silver pieces had no lines bordering the six-pointed star. From 1854 through 1858 there were three lines, while issues of the last fifteen years show only two lines. Issues from 1854 through 1873 have an olive sprig over the III and a bundle of three arrows beneath.

UNCIRCULATED
Absolutely no trace of wear.

A coin exactly as it was minted, with no trace of wear or injury. May lack full mint luster, and surface may be dull or spotted.

Check points for signs of abrasion: points and ridges of star; high parts of Roman numeral III.

ABOUT UNCIRCULATED
Small trace of wear visible on highest points.

OBVERSE: Traces of wear show on star ridges and points. Edges are distinct on five of the six star points.

REVERSE: Traces of wear show on leaves and Roman numeral.
Half of the mint luster is still present.

EXTREMELY FINE
Very light wear on only the highest points.

THREE CENTS—SILVER 1851-1873

OBVERSE: Slight wear shows on outer edge of the shield. High points of the star points and ridges are worn but show all details.

REVERSE: Entire central design is lightly worn but all details are visible.

VERY FINE
Light to moderate even wear. All major features are sharp.

OBVERSE: Shield shows considerable flatness, but all features are clear. Over half the details show in star edges. Legend worn but bold.

REVERSE: Numeral, C, and stars are worn. Design within C is all visible.

FINE
Moderate to heavy even wear. Entire design clear and bold.

OBVERSE: Some details show in scroll and outer shield lines; central shield lines are nearly all visible. The entire star is plain but very weak.

REVERSE: All details are visible in the C. Numeral is very smooth and stars are well worn.

VERY GOOD
Well worn. Design clear but flat and lacking details.

THREE CENTS—SILVER 1851–1873

OBVERSE: Outline of star and shield show but parts are smooth. Shield lines are weak and incomplete. Only a few vertical shield lines show separations.

REVERSE: Design in C is complete but very weak. Numeral and stars well worn but fully outlined. Most of rim is visible.

GOOD
Heavily worn. Design and legend visible but faint in spots.

OBVERSE: Entire design well worn with very little detail remaining. Half the shield lines are weak but visible. Rim merges with legend.

REVERSE: Design is worn nearly flat but is completely outlined. Design in C is weak but visible. Stars merge with rim.

ABOUT GOOD
Outlined design. Parts of date and legend worn smooth.

OBVERSE: Design is outlined with nearly all details worn away. Date and legend readable but very weak and merging into rim.

REVERSE: Entire design partially worn away. Rim is merged with the stars. Only parts of the design in C are visible.

THREE CENTS—NICKEL 1865–1889

UNCIRCULATED
Absolutely no trace of wear.

A coin exactly as it was minted, with no trace of wear or injury. May lack full mint luster, and surface may be dull or spotted. May have some weakness in LIBERTY or on the numeral III.

Check points for signs of abrasion: high points of cheek, hair curls, and hair above forehead.

ABOUT UNCIRCULATED
Small trace of wear visible on highest points.

OBVERSE: Traces of wear show on the curls and hair above forehead.

REVERSE: Traces of wear show on wreath and numeral III.
 Part of the mint luster is still present.

EXTREMELY FINE
Very light wear on only the highest points.

OBVERSE: Wear shows on hair above forehead, on the cheek, and on curls.

REVERSE: High points of wheat leaves are worn, but each line is clearly defined. Numeral shows some wear.

THREE CENTS—NICKEL 1865–1889

VERY FINE
Light to moderate even wear. All major features are sharp.

OBVERSE: Over half the details still show in hair and curls. Head worn but bold. Coronet is partially beaded on upper edge.

REVERSE: Leaves are worn but some of the ribs are visible. Most of the lines in the numeral are clear unless weakly struck.

FINE
Moderate to heavy even wear. Entire design clear and bold.

OBVERSE: Some details show in curls and hair at top of ear. Beading worn smooth at top of coronet.

REVERSE: Some details visible in wreath. About half the lines in the numeral are clear.

VERY GOOD
Well worn. Design clear but flat and lacking details.

OBVERSE: Top edge of coronet and most hair details are worn smooth. Legend and date are clear. Rim is complete.

REVERSE: Slight detail in wreath shows, but half the leaves are separated. Some lines in the numeral are visible. Rim is complete.

THREE CENTS—NICKEL 1865–1889

GOOD
Heavily worn. Design and legend visible but faint in spots.

OBVERSE: Entire design well worn with very little detail remaining. Legend and date are weak but visible.

REVERSE: Wreath is worn flat but completely outlined. Roman numeral is worn smooth.

ABOUT GOOD
Outlined design. Parts of date and legend worn smooth.

OBVERSE: Head is outlined with nearly all details worn away. Legend and date readable but very weak and merging into rim.

REVERSE: Entire design partially worn away. Rim is merged with the wreath.

NICKEL FIVE CENTS—SHIELD 1866–1883

UNCIRCULATED
Absolutely no trace of wear.

A coin exactly as it was minted, with no trace of wear or injury. May lack full mint luster, and surface may be dull or spotted.

Check points for signs of abrasion: tips of leaves; high points of shield. Shallow or weak spots in the relief, particularly in the numeral 5, are usually caused by improper striking and not wear.

ABOUT UNCIRCULATED
Small trace of wear visible on highest points.

OBVERSE: Traces of wear show on the cross and at tips of the leaves.

REVERSE: Traces of wear show on numeral and stars.
Traces of mint luster still show.

EXTREMELY FINE
Very light wear on only the highest points.

OBVERSE: Cross is lightly worn but well defined and bold. Slight wear shows on horizontal lines of the shield. High points of leaves are worn but show all details.

REVERSE: Numeral and stars are worn but all details are visible.

NICKEL FIVE CENTS—SHIELD 1866–1883

VERY FINE
Light to moderate even wear. All major features are sharp.

OBVERSE: Shield shows considerable flatness, but half of the horizontal lines are clear. Parts of the details still show in leaves. Cross worn but outlined.
REVERSE: Numeral and stars are worn. Star centers show half of details.

FINE
Moderate to heavy even wear. Entire design clear and bold.

OBVERSE: Some details show in leaves and shield lines. The entire motto is plain but very weak.

REVERSE: Some details visible in stars. Numeral is very smooth but distinct.

VERY GOOD
Well worn. Design clear but flat and lacking details.

OBVERSE: Outline of leaves and cross show but parts are smooth. Motto is weak but visible. Only a few vertical shield lines show separations.

REVERSE: Slight detail shows in stars. The rim is clear. Numeral is worn nearly flat but is completely outlined.

NICKEL FIVE CENTS—SHIELD 1866–1883

GOOD
Heavily worn. Design and legend visible but faint in spots.

OBVERSE: Entire design is well worn with very little detail remaining. Motto is weak and incomplete.

REVERSE: Numeral nearly flat but is outlined. Legend is weak but readable. Rim worn to tops of letters.

ABOUT GOOD
Outlined design. Parts of date and legend worn smooth.

OBVERSE: Design is outlined with nearly all details worn away. Date and motto partially readable but very weak and merging into rim.

REVERSE: Entire design partially worn away. Rim is merged with the letters. Only parts of stars and legend are visible.

UNCIRCULATED
Absolutely no trace of wear.

A coin exactly as it was minted, with no trace of wear or injury. May lack full mint luster, and surface may be dull or spotted.

Check points for signs of abrasion: high points of hair left of ear and at forehead. Corn ears at bottom of wreath.

ABOUT UNCIRCULATED
Small trace of wear visible on highest points.

OBVERSE: Traces of wear show on hair left of ear and at forehead.

REVERSE: Traces of wear show on the wreath and on corn ears.
Part of the mint luster is still present.

EXTREMELY FINE
Very light wear on only the highest points.

OBVERSE: Wear shows on hair from forehead to ear, on the cheek, and on curls.

REVERSE: High points of wreath are worn, but each line is clearly defined. Corn shows some wear.

NICKEL FIVE CENTS—LIBERTY HEAD 1883–1912
VERY FINE
Light to moderate even wear. All major features are sharp.

OBVERSE: Over half the details still show in hair and curls. Head worn but bold. Every letter on coronet is plainly visible.

REVERSE: Leaves are worn but some of the ribs are visible. Most details in the wreath are clear unless weakly struck.

FINE
Moderate to heavy even wear. Entire design clear and bold.

OBVERSE: Some details show in curls and hair at top of head. All letters of LIBERTY are visible.

REVERSE: Some details visible in wreath. Letters in the motto are worn but clear.

VERY GOOD
Well worn. Design clear but flat and lacking details.

OBVERSE: Bottom edge of coronet, and most hair details, are worn smooth. At least three letters in LIBERTY are clear. Rim is complete.

REVERSE: Wreath shows only bold outline. Some letters in the motto are very weak. Rim is complete.

GOOD
Heavily worn. Design and legend visible but faint in spots.

OBVERSE: Entire design well worn with very little detail remaining. Stars and date are weak but visible.

REVERSE: Wreath is worn flat and not completely outlined. Legend and motto are worn nearly smooth.

ABOUT GOOD
Outlined design. Parts of date and legend worn smooth.

OBVERSE: Head is outlined with nearly all details worn away. Date readable but very weak and merging into rim.

REVERSE: Entire design partially worn away.

NICKEL FIVE CENTS—BUFFALO 1913–1938

UNCIRCULATED
Absolutely no trace of wear.

A coin exactly as it was minted, with no trace of wear or injury. May lack full mint luster and surface may be dull or spotted.

Check points for signs of abrasion: high points of Indian's cheek. Upper front leg, hip, tip of tail. Shallow or weak spots in the relief are usually caused by improper striking and not wear.

ABOUT UNCIRCULATED
Small trace of wear visible on highest points.

OBVERSE: Traces of wear show on hair above and to left of forehead, and at the cheek bone.

REVERSE: Traces of wear show on tail, hip and hair above and around the horn.

Traces of mint luster still show.

EXTREMELY FINE
Very light wear on only the highest points.

OBVERSE: Hair and face are lightly worn but well defined and bold. Slight wear shows on lines of hair braid.

REVERSE: Horn and end of tail are worn but all details are visible.

NICKEL FIVE CENTS—BUFFALO 1913–1938

VERY FINE
Light to moderate even wear. All major features are sharp.

OBVERSE: Hair and cheek show considerable flatness, but all details are clear. Feathers still show partial detail.

REVERSE: Hair on head is worn. Tail and point of horn are visible.

FINE
Moderate to considerable even wear. Entire design clear and bold.

OBVERSE: Three-quarters of details show in hair and braid. LIBERTY is plain but merging with rim.

REVERSE: Major details visible along the back. Horn and tail are smooth but three-quarters visible.

VERY GOOD
Well worn. Design clear but flat and lacking details.

OBVERSE: Outline of hair is visible at temple and near cheek bone. LIBERTY merges with rim. Date is clear.

REVERSE: Some detail shows in head. Lettering is all clear. Horn is worn nearly flat but is partially visible.

NICKEL FIVE CENTS—BUFFALO 1913–1938

GOOD
Heavily worn. Design and legend visible but faint in spots.

OBVERSE: Entire design well worn with very little detail remaining in central part. LIBERTY is weak and merged with rim.

REVERSE: Buffalo is nearly flat but is well outlined. Horn does not show. Legend is weak but readable. Rim worn to tops of letters.

ABOUT GOOD
Outlined design. Parts of date and legend worn smooth.

OBVERSE: Design is outlined with nearly all details worn away. Date and motto partially readable but very weak and merging into rim.

REVERSE: Entire design partially worn away. Rim is merged with the letters.

NICKEL FIVE CENTS—JEFFERSON 1938 TO DATE

UNCIRCULATED
Absolutely no trace of wear.

A coin exactly as it was minted, with no trace of wear or injury. May lack full mint luster, and surface may be dull or spotted.

Check points for signs of abrasion: cheek bone and high points of hair. Triangular roof above pillars. Shallow or weak spots in the relief, particularly in the steps below pillars, are usually caused by improper striking and no wear.

ABOUT UNCIRCULATED
Small trace of wear visible on highest points.

OBVERSE: Traces of wear show on cheek bone and high points of hair.

REVERSE: Traces of wear show on the beam and triangular roof above pillars. Half of the mint luster is still present.

EXTREMELY FINE
Very light wear on only the highest points.

OBVERSE: Hair is lightly worn but well defined and bold. Slight wear show on cheek bone and bottom of the bust. High points of hair are worn but show all details.

REVERSE: Triangular roof and beam are worn but all details are visible.

NICKEL FIVE CENTS—JEFFERSON 1938 TO DATE

VERY FINE
Light to moderate even wear. All major features are sharp.

OBVERSE: Cheek line shows considerable flatness. Over half the hair lines are clear. Parts of the details still show in collar.

REVERSE: Pillars are worn but clearly defined. Triangular roof is partially visible.

FINE
Moderate to heavy even wear. Entire design clear and bold.

OBVERSE: Some details show in hair around face. Cheek line and collar plain but very weak.

REVERSE: Some details visible behind pillars. Triangular roof is very smooth and indistinct.

VERY GOOD
Well worn. Design clear but flat and lacking details.

OBVERSE: Cheek line is visible but parts are worn smooth. Collar is weak but visible. Only a few hair lines show separations.

REVERSE: Slight detail shows throughout building. The arch is worn away. Pillars are weak but visible.

NICKEL FIVE CENTS—JEFFERSON 1938 TO DAT

GOOD
Heavily worn. Design and legend visible but faint in spots.

OBVERSE: Entire design well worn with very little detail remaining. Motto weak and merged with rim.

REVERSE: Building is nearly flat but is well outlined. Pillars are worn fla Rim worn to tops of letters.

ABOUT GOOD
Outlined design. Parts of date and legend worn smooth.

OBVERSE: Design is outlined with nearly all details worn away. Date an legend readable but very weak and merging into rim.

REVERSE: Entire design partially worn away. Rim is merged with the letter

HALF DIMES—HERALDIC EAGLE 1800–1805

UNCIRCULATED
Absolutely no trace of wear.

A coin exactly as it was minted, with no trace of wear or injury. May lack full mint luster, and surface may be dull, spotted or heavily toned.

Check points for signs of abrasion: high points of bust, shoulder, and hair above ear and at forehead; eagle's head and top edges of wings. Shallow or weak spots in the relief are usually caused by improper striking and not wear.

ABOUT UNCIRCULATED
Small trace of wear visible on highest points.

OBVERSE: Traces of wear show on hair above forehead. Drapery has trace of wear at shoulder and bustline.

REVERSE: Traces of wear show on shield, head, and top wing edges.
   Half of the mint luster is still present.

EXTREMELY FINE
Very light wear on only the highest points.

OBVERSE: Wear shows on hair from forehead to ear, and lightly on the cheek. Drapery lightly worn at neckline in spots.

REVERSE: High points of the eagle are worn, but each detail is clearly defined. Tail and feathers above shield are very weak.
   Traces of mint luster may still show.

HALF DIMES—HERALDIC EAGLE 1800–1805
VERY FINE
Light to moderate even wear. All major features are sharp.

OBVERSE: Hair above forehead worn almost smooth. Three-quarters of the details still show in flowing hair. Every letter and star is plainly visible. Left side of drapery is indistinct.

REVERSE: Head and tail are worn, but some of the feathers are visible. Most of the details in wings are clear unless weakly struck. The motto is weak but complete.

FINE
Moderate to heavy even wear. Entire design clear and bold.

OBVERSE: Some details show in hair ends, and at left of ear. All letters, date and stars are visible.

REVERSE: Half the feathers are visible in wings. Letters in legend are worn but clear. Parts of motto are very weak.

VERY GOOD
Well worn. Design clear but flat and lacking details.

OBVERSE: Entire head is weak, and most hair details are worn smooth. Date and LIBERTY are weak but clear.

REVERSE: Eagle shows bold outline with only a few feathers visible. Some letters in legend are very weak. Motto is only partially visible.

HALF DIMES—HERALDIC EAGLE 1800–1805

GOOD
Heavily worn. Design and legend visible but faint in spots.

OBVERSE: Entire design well worn with very little detail remaining. Legend, stars and date are weak but visible.

REVERSE: Eagle is worn flat but is completely outlined. Tops of some letters, head, and motto are worn nearly smooth.

ABOUT GOOD
Outlined design. Parts of date and legend worn smooth.

OBVERSE: Head is outlined with nearly all details worn away. Date readable but very weak. Stars merging into rim.

REVERSE: Entire design partially worn away.

HALF DIMES—CAPPED BUST 1829–1837
UNCIRCULATED
Absolutely no trace of wear.

A coin exactly as it was minted, with no trace of wear or injury. May lac[k] full mint luster, and surface may be dull, spotted or heavily toned.

Check points for signs of abrasion: drapery at tip of bust, shoulder clasp and hair above eye and at forehead. Eagle's claws, neck, and edges of wings. Shallow or weak spots in the motto are usually caused by improper striking and not wear.

ABOUT UNCIRCULATED
Small trace of wear visible on highest points.

OBVERSE: Traces of wear show on hair above eye and over the ear. Draper[y] has trace of wear at tip of bust.

REVERSE: Traces of wear show on talons, head, and edges of wings.
Half of the mint luster is still present.

EXTREMELY FINE
Very light wear on only the highest points.

OBVERSE: Wear shows on hair above eye and ear, and lightly on curls. Drapery lightly worn at neckline in spots. The eye and shoulder clasp are ver[y] sharp.

HALF DIMES—CAPPED BUST 1829–1837

REVERSE: High points of the eagle are worn, but each detail is clearly defined. Head, neck feathers, and leg feathers are very lightly worn.

Traces of mint luster may still show.

VERY FINE
Light to moderate even wear. All major features are sharp.

OBVERSE: Over half the details still show in hair. Drapery and lower curls worn but bold. Ear, clasp and star centers are all plainly visible.

REVERSE: Head and leg are worn, but some feathers are visible. Most of the details in the wings are clear unless weakly struck. Motto is complete.

FINE
Moderate to heavy even wear. Entire design clear and bold.

OBVERSE: About half the details show in hair ends, and at left of ear. All letters, and parts of ear and clasp are visible.

REVERSE: Half of the feathers are visible in the wings. Letters in motto are worn but clear.

VERY GOOD
Well worn. Design clear but flat and lacking details.

HALF DIMES—CAPPED BUST 1829–1837

OBVERSE: Entire head is weak, and most hair details are worn smooth. Date and LIBERTY are weak but clear.

REVERSE: Eagle is boldly outlined with some feathers showing in wings. Some letters in the motto are very weak or partially missing.

GOOD
Heavily worn. Design and legend visible but faint in spots.

OBVERSE: Entire design well worn with very little detail remaining. Half the letters in LIBERTY are worn away. Stars and date are weak but visible.

REVERSE: Eagle is worn nearly flat but is completely outlined. Tops of some letters are worn nearly smooth and may merge with rim.

ABOUT GOOD
Outlined design. Parts of date and legend worn smooth.

OBVERSE: Head is outlined with nearly all details worn away. Date readable but very weak. Stars merging into rim.

REVERSE: Entire design partially worn away.

HALF DIMES—LIBERTY SEATED 1837-1859

UNCIRCULATED
Absolutely no trace of wear.

A coin exactly as it was minted, with no trace of wear or injury. May lack full mint luster, and surface may be dull, spotted or heavily toned.

Check points for signs of abrasion: high points of breast and knees. Ribbon bow and tips of leaves. Weak spots in the horizontal shield lines are usually caused by striking and not wear.

ABOUT UNCIRCULATED
Small trace of wear visible on highest points.

OBVERSE: Traces of wear show on knees, right shoulder and hairline.

REVERSE: Traces of wear show on ribbon bow, and tips of leaves.
    Half of the mint luster is still present.

EXTREMELY FINE
Very light wear on only the highest points.

OBVERSE: Wear shows on knees, head and shoulder. Gown lightly worn at neckline in spots. LIBERTY is complete and scroll edges are raised.

REVERSE: High points of wreath and bow are worn, but all details are clearly defined.
    Traces of mint luster may still show.

HALF DIMES—LIBERTY SEATED 1837–1859

VERY FINE
Light to moderate even wear. All major features are sharp.

OBVERSE: Over half the details still show in the gown. Hair worn but bold. Every letter in LIBERTY is visible.

REVERSE: The ribbon is worn, but some details are visible. Half the details in the leaves are clear.

FINE
Moderate to heavy even wear. Entire design clear and bold.

OBVERSE: Some details show in cap and at the shoulder and breast. All letters in LIBERTY are weak but visible.

REVERSE: Half the details in leaves are visible. Bow is outlined but flat. Letters in the legend are worn but clear.

VERY GOOD
Well worn. Design clear but flat and lacking details.

OBVERSE: Entire shield is weak, and most of the gown details are worn smooth. Three letters in LIBERTY are clear.

REVERSE: Wreath shows only bold outline. Some of the bow is very weak.

GOOD
Heavily worn. Design and legend visible but faint in spots.

OBVERSE: Entire design well worn with very little detail remaining. Date is weak but visible.

REVERSE: Wreath is worn flat but is completely outlined. Tops of some letters are worn nearly smooth.

ABOUT GOOD
Outlined design. Parts of date and legend worn smooth.

OBVERSE: Liberty is outlined with nearly all details worn away. Date readable but very weak. Stars merging into rim.

REVERSE: Entire design partially worn away.

HALF DIMES—LIBERTY SEATED 1860–1873

UNCIRCULATED
Absolutely no trace of wear.

A coin exactly as it was minted, with no trace of wear or injury. May lack full mint luster, and surface may be dull, spotted, or heavily toned.

Check points for signs of abrasion: high points of breast and knees. Ribbon bow and tips of leaves.

ABOUT UNCIRCULATED
Small trace of wear visible on highest points.

OBVERSE: Traces of wear show on knees, right shoulder, and edge of hairline.

REVERSE: Traces of wear show on ribbon bow, and tips of leaves.
    Half of the mint luster is still present.

EXTREMELY FINE
Very light wear on only the highest points.

OBVERSE: Wear shows on knees, head and shoulder. Gown lightly worn at neckline in spots. LIBERTY is complete and scroll edges are raised.

REVERSE: High points of wreath and bow are worn, but all details are clearly defined.
    Traces of mint luster may still show.

HALF DIMES—LIBERTY SEATED 1860–1873
VERY FINE
Light to moderate even wear. All major features are sharp.

OBVERSE: Over half the details still show in the gown. Hair worn but bold. Every letter in LIBERTY is visible. Details in cap are visible.

REVERSE: The ribbon is worn, but some of the details are visible. Half the details in the leaves are clear. Bottom leaves and upper stalks show wear spots.

FINE
Moderate to heavy even wear. Entire design clear and bold.

OBVERSE: Some details show in cap and at the shoulder and breast. All letters in LIBERTY are weak but visible. Clasp is worn away.

REVERSE: Some details in the upper leaves and corn are visible. Bow is nearly all outlined but flat. Letters in legend are worn but clear.

VERY GOOD
Well worn. Design clear but flat and lacking details.

OBVERSE: Entire shield is weak, and most details in the gown, knee and legs are worn smooth. Three letters in LIBERTY are clear. Rim is complete.

REVERSE: Wreath shows only a small amount of detail. Corn and grain are flat. Some of the bow merges with wreath.

HALF DIMES—LIBERTY SEATED 1860–1873

GOOD
Heavily worn. Design and legend visible but faint in spots.

OBVERSE: Entire design well worn with very little detail remaining. Date is weak but visible. LIBERTY is worn away.

REVERSE: Wreath is worn flat but is completely outlined. Corn and grains are worn nearly smooth.

ABOUT GOOD
Outlined design. Parts of date and legend worn smooth.

OBVERSE: Liberty is outlined with nearly all details worn away. Date readable but worn. Legend merging into rim.

REVERSE: Entire design partially worn away.

DIMES—HERALDIC EAGLE 1798–1807

UNCIRCULATED
Absolutely no trace of wear.

A coin exactly as it was minted, with no trace of wear or injury. May lack full mint luster, and surface may be dull, spotted or heavily toned.

Check points for signs of abrasion: high points of bust, shoulder, and hair above ear and at forehead; eagle's head and top edges of wings. Shallow or weak spots in the relief are usually caused by improper striking and not wear.

ABOUT UNCIRCULATED
Small trace of wear visible on highest points.

OBVERSE: Traces of wear show on hair above ear and at forehead. Drapery has trace of wear at shoulder and bustline.

REVERSE: Traces of wear show on shield, head, tail, and the top edges of wings.

Half of the mint luster is still present.

EXTREMELY FINE
Very light wear on only the highest points.

OBVERSE: Wear shows on hair from forehead to ear, and lightly on the cheek. Drapery lightly worn at neckline in spots.

REVERSE: High points of the eagle are worn, but each detail is clearly defined. Tail and feathers above shield are very weak.

Traces of mint luster may still show.

DIMES—HERALDIC EAGLE 1798–1807
VERY FINE
Light to moderate even wear. All major features are sharp.

OBVERSE: Hair above forehead worn almost smooth. Three-quarters of the details still show in flowing hair. Every letter and star is plainly visible. Left side of drapery is indistinct.

REVERSE: Head and tail are worn, but some of the feathers are visible. Most of the details in wings are clear unless weakly struck. The motto is weak but complete.

FINE
Moderate to heavy even wear. Entire design clear and bold.

OBVERSE: Some details show in hair ends, and at left of ear. All letters, date and stars are visible.

REVERSE: Half the feathers are visible in the wings. Letters in legend are worn but clear. Parts of motto are very weak.

VERY GOOD
Well worn. Design clear but flat and lacking details.

OBVERSE: Entire head is weak, and most hair details are worn smooth. Date and LIBERTY are weak but clear.

REVERSE: Eagle shows bold outline with only a few feathers visible. Some of the letters in legend are very weak. Motto is only partially visible.

[74]

DIMES—HERALDIC EAGLE 1798–1807

GOOD
Heavily worn. Design and legend visible but faint in spots.

OBVERSE: Entire design well worn with very little detail remaining. Legend, stars and date are weak but visible.

REVERSE: Eagle is worn flat but is completely outlined. Tops of some letters, head, and motto are worn nearly smooth.

ABOUT GOOD
Outlined design. Parts of date and legend worn smooth.

OBVERSE: Head is outlined with nearly all details worn away. Date readable but very weak. Stars merging into rim.

REVERSE: Entire design partially worn away.

DIMES—CAPPED BUST 1809–1837

UNCIRCULATED
Absolutely no trace of wear.

A coin exactly as it was minted, with no trace of wear or injury. May lack full mint luster, and surface may be dull, spotted, or heavily toned.

Check points for signs of abrasion: drapery at front of bust, shoulder clasp, and hair above ear and at forehead. Eagle's claws, neck, and edges of wings. Shallow or weak spots in the design are usually caused by improper striking and not wear.

ABOUT UNCIRCULATED
Small trace of wear visible on highest points.

OBVERSE: Traces of wear show on hair above eye and over the ear. Drapery has trace of wear at tip of bust.

REVERSE: Traces of wear show on talons, head, and edges of wings.
Half of the mint luster is still present.

EXTREMELY FINE
Very light wear on only the highest points.

OBVERSE: Wear shows on hair above eye and ear, and lightly on the curls. Drapery lightly worn at neckline in spots. The ear and shoulder clasp are very sharp. Eye is well defined.

DIMES—CAPPED BUST 1809–1837

REVERSE: High points of the eagle are worn, but each detail is clearly defined. Neck and leg feathers are very lightly worn. Talons and olive branch show slight wear.

Traces of mint luster may still show.

VERY FINE
Light to moderate even wear. All major features are sharp.

OBVERSE: Over half the details still show in hair. Drapery and lower curls worn but bold. Ear, clasp and LIBERTY are all plainly visible.

REVERSE: Head and leg are worn, but some of the feathers are visible. Most details in the wings are clear unless weakly struck. Motto is complete. Talons are separated.

FINE
Moderate to heavy even wear. Entire design clear and bold.

OBVERSE: Nearly half the details show in hair, drapery, and cap. All letters, and parts of ear and clasp are visible. Eyelid is flattened. Parts of rim are worn flat.

REVERSE: Half the feathers are visible in the wings. Letters in the motto are weak but clear. Head is nearly smooth but eye and some feathers show.

VERY GOOD
Well worn. Design clear but flat and lacking details.

DIMES—CAPPED BUST 1809–1837

OBVERSE: Entire head outlined with most hair details worn smooth. Eye, ear, and clasp are barely visible. At least three letters in LIBERTY are clear.

REVERSE: Eagle is boldly outlined with some feathers showing in wings. Some of the letters in motto are very weak. Head and olive branch are smooth.

GOOD
Heavily worn. Design and legend visible but faint in spots.

OBVERSE: Entire design well worn with very little detail remaining. Most of the letters in LIBERTY are worn away. Stars and date are weak but visible and may merge with rim.

REVERSE: Eagle is worn nearly flat but is completely outlined. Tops of some letters are worn nearly smooth and may merge with rim. Eye and motto are only partially visible.

ABOUT GOOD
Outlined design. Parts of date and legend worn smooth.

OBVERSE: Head is outlined with nearly all details worn away. Date readable but very weak. Stars merging into rim.

REVERSE: Entire design partially worn away.

DIMES—LIBERTY SEATED 1837–1859
UNCIRCULATED
Absolutely no trace of wear.

A coin exactly as it was minted, with no trace of wear or injury. May lack full mint luster, and surface may be dull, spotted, or heavily toned.

Check points for signs of abrasion: high points of breast and knees. Ribbon bow and tips of leaves. Weak spots in the design are usually caused by striking and not wear.

ABOUT UNCIRCULATED
Small trace of wear visible on highest points.

OBVERSE: Traces of wear show on knees, right shoulder, and edge of hairline.

REVERSE: Traces of wear show on ribbon bow, and tips of leaves.
    Half of the mint luster is still present.

EXTREMELY FINE
Very light wear on only the highest points.

OBVERSE: Wear shows on knees, head and shoulder. Gown lightly worn at neckline in spots. LIBERTY is complete and scroll edges are raised.

REVERSE: High points of wreath and bow are worn, but all details are clearly defined.

    Traces of mint luster may still show.

DIMES—LIBERTY SEATED 1837–1859

VERY FINE
Light to moderate even wear. All major features are sharp.

OBVERSE: Over half the details still show in the gown. Hair, shoulder, and legs are worn but bold. Every letter in LIBERTY is visible.

REVERSE: The ribbon is worn, but some details are visible. Half the details in the leaves are clear.

FINE
Moderate to heavy even wear. Entire design clear and bold.

OBVERSE: Some details show in hair, cap, and at the shoulder and breast. All letters in LIBERTY are weak but visible.

REVERSE: Some of the details in leaves are visible. Bow is outlined but flat. Leaves are separated. Letters in legend are worn but clear.

VERY GOOD
Well worn. Design clear but flat and lacking details.

OBVERSE: Entire shield is weak, and most gown details are worn smooth. Three letters in LIBERTY are clear. Rim is complete.

REVERSE: Wreath shows only bold outline. Some of the bow is very weak.

GOOD
Heavily worn. Design and legend visible but faint in spots.

OBVERSE: Entire design well worn with very little detail remaining. Date is weak but visible.

REVERSE: Wreath is worn flat but is completely outlined. Tops of some letters are worn nearly smooth.

ABOUT GOOD
Outlined design. Parts of date and legend worn smooth.

OBVERSE: Liberty is outlined with nearly all details worn away. Date readable but very weak. Stars merging into rim.

REVERSE: Entire design partially worn away.

DIMES—LIBERTY SEATED 1860–1891
UNCIRCULATED
Absolutely no trace of wear.

A coin exactly as it was minted, with no trace of wear or injury. May lack full mint luster, and surface may be dull, spotted, or heavily toned.

Check points for signs of abrasion: high points of breast and knees. Ribbon bow and tips of leaves.

ABOUT UNCIRCULATED
Small trace of wear visible on highest points.

OBVERSE: Traces of wear show on knees, right shoulder, and edge of hairline.

REVERSE: Traces of wear show on ribbon bow, and tips of leaves.
Half of the mint luster is still present.

EXTREMELY FINE
Very light wear on only the highest points.

OBVERSE: Wear shows on knees, head and shoulder. Gown lightly worn at neckline in spots. LIBERTY is complete and scroll edges are raised.

REVERSE: High points of wreath and bow are worn, but all details are clearly defined.
Traces of mint luster may still show.

DIMES—LIBERTY SEATED 1860–1891

VERY FINE
Light to moderate even wear. All major features are sharp.

OBVERSE: Over half the details still show in the gown. Hair, shoulder, and legs are worn but bold. Every letter in LIBERTY is visible. Details in cap are visible.

REVERSE: The ribbon is worn, but some details are visible. Half of the details in leaves are clear. Bottom leaves and upper stalks show wear spots.

FINE
Moderate to heavy even wear. Entire design clear and bold.

OBVERSE: Some details show in hair, cap, and at the shoulder and breast. All letters in LIBERTY are weak but visible. Clasp is worn away.

REVERSE: Some details in upper leaves and corn are visible. Bow is outlined but flat. Letters in legend are worn but clear.

VERY GOOD
Well worn. Design clear but flat and lacking details.

OBVERSE: Entire shield is weak, and most details in the gown, knee and legs are worn smooth. Three letters in LIBERTY are clear. Rim is complete.

REVERSE: Wreath shows only a small amount of details. Corn and grain are flat. Some of the bow is very weak.

DIMES—LIBERTY SEATED 1860–1891

GOOD
Heavily worn. Design and legend visible but faint in spots.

OBVERSE: Entire design well worn with very little detail remaining. Date is weak but visible. LIBERTY is worn away.

REVERSE: Wreath is worn flat but is completely outlined. Corn and grain are worn nearly smooth.

ABOUT GOOD
Outlined design. Parts of date and legend worn smooth.

OBVERSE: Liberty is outlined with nearly all details worn away. Date readable but worn. Legend merging into rim.

REVERSE: Entire design partially worn away.

DIMES—BARBER 1892–1916
UNCIRCULATED
Absolutely no trace of wear.

A coin exactly as it was minted, with no trace of wear or injury. May lack full mint luster, and surface may be dull, spotted, or heavily toned.

Check points for signs of abrasion; high points of cheek, and hair below LIBERTY. Ribbon bow and tips of leaves.

ABOUT UNCIRCULATED
Small trace of wear visible on highest points.

OBVERSE: Traces of wear show on cheek, top of forehead, and hair below LIBERTY.

REVERSE: Traces of wear show on ribbon bow, wheat grains, and tips of leaves.

Half of the mint luster is still present.

EXTREMELY FINE
Very light wear on only the highest points.

OBVERSE: Light wear shows on leaves, cheek, cap and hair above forehead. LIBERTY is sharp and band edges are clear.

REVERSE: High points of wreath and bow are worn, but all details are clearly defined.

Traces of mint luster may still show.

DIMES—BARBER 1892–1916

VERY FINE
Light to moderate even wear. All major features are sharp.

OBVERSE: Over half the details still show in leaves. Hair worn but bold. Every letter in LIBERTY is visible.

REVERSE: The ribbon is worn, but some details are visible. Half the details in leaves are clear. Bottom leaves and upper stalks show wear spots.

FINE
Moderate to heavy even wear. Entire design clear and bold.

OBVERSE: Some details show in hair, cap, and facial features. All letters in LIBERTY are weak but visible. Upper row of leaves is outlined, but bottom row is worn smooth.

REVERSE: Some details in the lower leaf clusters are plainly visible. Bow is outlined but flat. Letters in legend are worn but clear.

VERY GOOD
Well worn. Design clear but flat and lacking details.

OBVERSE: Entire head weak, and most of the details in the face are worn smooth. Three letters in LIBERTY are clear. Rim is complete.

REVERSE: Wreath shows only a small amount of detail. Corn and grain are flat. Some of the bow is very weak.

DIMES—BARBER 1892–1916

GOOD
Heavily worn. Design and legend visible but faint in spots.

OBVERSE: Entire design well worn with very little detail remaining. Legend is weak but visible. LIBERTY is worn away.

REVERSE: Wreath is worn flat but is completely outlined. Corn and grains are worn nearly smooth.

ABOUT GOOD
Outlined design. Parts of date and legend worn smooth.

OBVERSE: Head is outlined with nearly all details worn away. Date readable but partially worn away. Legend merging into rim.

REVERSE: Entire wreath partially worn away and merging into rim.

DIMES—MERCURY 1916–1945

UNCIRCULATED
Absolutely no trace of wear.

A coin exactly as it was minted, with no trace of wear or injury. May lack full mint luster, and surface may be dull, spotted, or heavily toned.

Check points for signs of abrasion: high points of hair and in front of ear. Diagonal bands on fasces.

ABOUT UNCIRCULATED
Small trace of wear visible on highest points.

OBVERSE: Traces of wear show on hair along face, above forehead, and in front of ear.

REVERSE: Traces of wear show on the fasces bands but edges are sharply defined.

Half of the mint luster is still present.

EXTREMELY FINE
Very light wear on only the highest points.

OBVERSE: Wear shows on high points of feathers, hair, and at neckline.

REVERSE: High points of fasces bands are worn, but all details are clearly defined and partially separated.

Traces of mint luster may still show.

DIMES—MERCURY 1916–1945

VERY FINE
Light to moderate even wear. All major features are sharp.

OBVERSE: Three-quarters of the details still show in feathers. Hair worn but bold. Some details in hair braid are visible.

REVERSE: Wear shows on the two diagonal bands but most details are visible. All vertical lines are sharp. All details in the branch are clear.

FINE
Moderate to considerable even wear. Entire design clear and bold.

OBVERSE: Some details show in hair. All feathers are weak but partially visible. Hair braid is nearly worn away.

REVERSE: Vertical lines are all visible but lack sharpness. Diagonal bands show on fasces but one is worn smooth at midpoint.

VERY GOOD
Well worn. Design clear but flat and lacking details.

OBVERSE: Entire head is weak, and most details in the wing are worn smooth. All letters and date are clear. Rim is complete.

REVERSE: About half the vertical lines in the fasces are visible. Rim is complete.

DIMES—MERCURY 1916–1945

GOOD
Heavily worn. Design and legend visible but faint in spots.

OBVERSE: Entire design well worn with very little detail remaining. Legend and date are weak but visible. Rim is visible.

REVERSE: Fasces is worn nearly flat but is completely outlined. Sticks and bands are worn smooth.

ABOUT GOOD
Outlined design. Parts of date and legend worn smooth.

OBVERSE: Head is outlined with nearly all details worn away. Date readable but worn. Legend merging into rim.

REVERSE: Entire design partially worn away. Rim worn half way into the legend.

DIMES—ROOSEVELT 1946 TO DATE

UNCIRCULATED
Absolutely no trace of wear.

A coin exactly as it was minted, with no trace of wear or injury. Has full mint luster, but surface may be dull, spotted, or toned.

Check points for signs of abrasion: high points of cheek, and hair above ear. Tops of leaves, and details in flame.

ABOUT UNCIRCULATED
Small trace of wear visible on highest points.

OBVERSE: Traces of wear show on hair above ear.

REVERSE: Traces of wear show on flame but details are sharply defined. Half of the mint luster is still present.

EXTREMELY FINE
Very light wear on only the highest points.

OBVERSE: Wear shows on high points of hair, and at cheek line. Ear shows slight wear on the upper tip.

REVERSE: High points of flame, torch, and leaves are worn, but all details are clearly defined and partially separated.

Traces of mint luster may still show.

DIMES—ROOSEVELT 1946 TO DATE
VERY FINE
Light to moderate even wear. All major features are sharp.

OBVERSE: Three-quarters of the details still show in hair. Face worn but bold. Some details in the ear are visible.

REVERSE: Wear shows on the flame but a few lines are visible. All torch lines are worn but bold. Most details in leaves are clear.

FINE
Moderate to heavy even wear. Entire design clear and bold.

OBVERSE: Half the details show in hair. All of the face is weak but boldly visible. Half of inner edge of ear is worn away.

REVERSE: Vertical lines are all visible, but horizontal bands are worn smooth. Leaves show some detail. Flame is nearly smooth.

VERY GOOD
Well worn. Design clear but flat and lacking details.

OBVERSE: Entire head is weak, and most of the details in hair and ear are worn smooth. All letters and date are clear. Rim is complete.

REVERSE: About half the outer vertical lines in torch are visible. Flame is only outlined. Leaves show very little detail. Rim is complete.

DIMES—ROOSEVELT 1946 TO DATE

GOOD
Heavily worn. Design and legend visible but faint in spots.

OBVERSE: Entire design well worn with very little detail remaining. Ear is completely outlined. Legend and date are weak but visible. Rim is visible.

REVERSE: Torch is worn nearly flat but is completely outlined. Leaves are worn smooth. Legend is all visible.

ABOUT GOOD
Outlined design. Parts of date and legend worn smooth.

OBVERSE: Head is outlined with nearly all details worn away. Date readable but worn. Legend merging into rim.

REVERSE: Entire design partially worn away. Rim merges into the legend.

TWENTY CENTS—1875–1878

UNCIRCULATED
Absolutely no trace of wear.

A coin exactly as it was minted, with no trace of wear or injury. May lack full mint luster, and surface may be dull, spotted, or heavily toned.

Check points for signs of abrasion: high points of the head, breast, and knees. Eagle's breast and top of wings.

ABOUT UNCIRCULATED
Small trace of wear visible on highest points.

OBVERSE: Traces of wear show on head, breast, knees, and arm. Clasp is very bold.

REVERSE: Traces of wear show on breast, and tops of wings.
Half of the mint luster is still present.

EXTREMELY FINE
Very light wear on only the highest points.

OBVERSE: Wear shows on knees, head, breast, arms and shoulder. LIBERTY is sharp and scroll edges are raised. Cap shows wear but details are plain.

REVERSE: High points of breast and head are worn, but all details are clearly defined. Wings show wear at top.
Traces of mint luster may still show.

TWENTY CENTS—1875–1878

VERY FINE
Light to moderate even wear. All major features are sharp.

OBVERSE: Less than half the details show in the hair. Head, shoulder, breast, and legs are worn but bold. Every letter in LIBERTY is visible.

REVERSE: Wings are worn, but three-quarters of the details are visible. Half the details in breast feathers are clear. Head is flat.

FINE
Moderate to heavy even wear. Entire design clear and bold.

OBVERSE: Some details show in gown, shield, and at the shoulder and breast. Three or more letters in LIBERTY must be visible. Clasp is worn. Head and hair are flat.

REVERSE: Half the details in wings and legs visible. Head is outlined but flat; eye is visible. Letters in legend are worn but clear.

VERY GOOD
Well worn. Design clear but flat and lacking details.

OBVERSE: Entire head is weak, and most details in the gown, knee and legs are worn smooth. One or two letters in LIBERTY may show. Some details show near right arm.

REVERSE: Breast shows only a small amount of detail. Eye is very weak. Head and wing edges are flat. Less than half the feathers are visible.

TWENTY CENTS—1875–1878

GOOD
Heavily worn. Design and legend visible but faint in spots.

OBVERSE: Entire design well worn with very little detail remaining. Shield is weak but partially visible. LIBERTY is worn away.

REVERSE: Eagle is worn flat but is completely outlined and some feathers are visible. Head and breast are worn nearly smooth.

ABOUT GOOD
Outlined design. Parts of date and legend worn smooth.

OBVERSE: Liberty is outlined with nearly all details worn away. Date readable but worn. Stars merging into rim.

REVERSE: Entire design partially worn away. Legend readable although merged with rim.

QUARTERS—HERALDIC EAGLE 1804–1807

UNCIRCULATED
Absolutely no trace of wear.

A coin exactly as it was minted, with no trace of wear or injury. May lack full mint luster, and surface may be dull, spotted or heavily toned.

Check points for signs of abrasion: high points of bust, shoulder, and hair above forehead; eagle's head and top edges of wings. Shallow or weak spots in the relief are usually caused by improper striking and not wear.

ABOUT UNCIRCULATED
Small trace of wear visible on highest points.

OBVERSE: Traces of wear show on hair above forehead. Drapery has trace of wear at shoulder and bustline.

REVERSE: Traces of wear show on head, tail, and top edges of wings.
 Half of the mint luster is still present.

EXTREMELY FINE
Very light wear on only the highest points.

OBVERSE: Wear shows on hair from forehead to ear, and lightly on the cheek and bust. Drapery lightly worn at neckline in spots.

REVERSE: High points of eagle are worn, but each detail is clearly defined. Tail and feathers above shield are very weak. Wear spots show on ribbon and clouds.
 Traces of mint luster may still show.

QUARTERS—HERALDIC EAGLE 1804–1807

VERY FINE
Light to moderate even wear. All major features are sharp.

OBVERSE: Hair above forehead worn almost smooth. Three-quarters of the details still show in flowing hair. Every letter and star is plainly visible. Left side of drapery is indistinct.

REVERSE: Head and tail are worn, but some feathers are visible. Most details in wings are clear unless weakly struck. The motto is weak but complete.

FINE
Moderate to heavy even wear. Entire design clear and bold.

OBVERSE: Some details show in drapery, hair ends, and at left of ear. All letters, date and stars are visible. Star centers are smooth.

REVERSE: Half the feathers are visible in wings. Letters in legend are worn but clear. Parts of motto are very weak. Tail feathers show separations.

VERY GOOD
Well worn. Design clear but flat and lacking details.

OBVERSE: Entire head is weak, and most hair details are worn smooth. Date and LIBERTY are weak but clear.

REVERSE: Eagle shows bold outline with only a few feathers visible. Some letters in legend are very weak. Motto is only partially visible.

GOOD
Heavily worn. Design and legend visible but faint in spots.

OBVERSE: Entire design well worn with very little detail remaining. Legend, stars and date are weak but visible.

REVERSE: Eagle is worn flat but is completely outlined. Tops of some letters, head, and motto are worn nearly smooth.

ABOUT GOOD
Outlined design. Parts of date and legend worn smooth.

OBVERSE: Head is outlined with nearly all details worn away. Date readable but very weak. Stars merging into rim.

REVERSE: Entire design partially worn away. Lettering merges with rim.

QUARTERS—CAPPED BUST 1815–1828
UNCIRCULATED
Absolutely no trace of wear.

A coin exactly as it was minted, with no trace of wear or injury. May lack full mint luster, and surface may be dull, spotted or heavily toned.

Check points for signs of abrasion: drapery at front of bust, shoulder clasp, and hair above eye and at tips of curls; eagle's claws, neck, and edges of wings.

ABOUT UNCIRCULATED
Small trace of wear visible on highest points.

OBVERSE: Traces of wear show on hair above eye and over the ear. Drapery clasp is clear and bold.

REVERSE: Traces of wear show on talons, arrowheads, and edges of wings. Half of the mint luster is still present.

EXTREMELY FINE
Very light wear on only the highest points.

OBVERSE: Wear shows on hair above eye and ear, and lightly on the cap and curls. Drapery lightly worn at neckline in spots. Ear and shoulder clasp are bold. Eye is well defined. Star details are complete.

REVERSE: High points of eagle are worn, but each detail is clearly defined. Neck and leg feathers are very lightly worn. Talons, arrows and olive branch show slight wear.

Traces of mint luster may still show.

QUARTERS—CAPPED BUST 1815–1828
VERY FINE
Light to moderate even wear. All major features are sharp.

OBVERSE: Over half of the details still show in hair. Drapery and lower curls worn but bold. Ear, clasp and curls are all plainly visible.

REVERSE: Head and leg are worn, but some feathers are visible. Most details in wings are clear unless weakly struck. Motto is complete. Half of the horizontal shield lines are separated.

FINE
Moderate to heavy even wear. Entire design clear and bold.

OBVERSE: Nearly half the details show in hair, drapery and cap. All letters, and parts of ear and clasp are visible. Eyelid is flattened. Parts of star centers are worn flat. LIBERTY is complete.

REVERSE: Half the feathers are visible in the wings. Letters in motto weak but clear. Head is nearly smooth; eye and some feathers show.

VERY GOOD
Well worn. Design clear but flat and lacking details.

OBVERSE: Entire head outlined with most hair details worn smooth. Eye, ear and clasp are barely visible. At least three letters in LIBERTY are clear. Star centers are flat.

REVERSE: Eagle is boldly outlined with some feathers showing in wings. Some letters in motto are very weak or partially worn away. Head, talons and olive branch are nearly smooth. Eye is visible.

QUARTERS—CAPPED BUST 1815–1828

GOOD
Heavily worn. Design and legend visible but faint in spots.

OBVERSE: Entire design well worn with very little detail remaining. Most of the letters in LIBERTY are worn away. Stars and date are weak but visible and may merge with rim.

REVERSE: Eagle is worn nearly flat but is completely outlined. Tops of some letters are worn nearly smooth and may merge with rim. Eye and motto are only partially visible.

ABOUT GOOD
Outlined design. Parts of date and legend worn smooth.

OBVERSE: Head is outlined with nearly all details worn away. Date readable but very weak. Stars merging into rim.

REVERSE: Entire design partially worn away.

UNCIRCULATED
Absolutely no trace of wear.

A coin exactly as it was minted, with no trace of wear or injury. May lack full mint luster, and surface may be dull, spotted or heavily toned.

Check points for signs of abrasion: top of cap, stars, and hair above ear and at forehead; eagle's claws, arrows, and edges of wings.

ABOUT UNCIRCULATED
Small trace of wear visible on highest points.

OBVERSE: Traces of wear show on the hair above eye and over the ear, at top of cap, and on the stars.

REVERSE: Traces of wear show on talons, arrowheads and edges of wings. Half of the mint luster is still present.

EXTREMELY FINE
Very light wear on only the highest points.

OBVERSE: Wear shows on hair above eye and ear, and lightly on the cap, curls and stars. Drapery lightly worn at neckline in spots. Ear and shoulder clasp are very sharp. Eye is well defined.

REVERSE: High points of eagle are worn, but each detail is clearly defined. Neck and leg feathers are very lightly worn. Talons, arrows and olive branch show slight wear.

Traces of mint luster may still show.

QUARTERS—CAPPED BUST 1831-1838

VERY FINE
Light to moderate even wear. All major features are sharp.

OBVERSE: Over half the details still show in hair. Drapery, cap and lower
curls worn but bold. Ear, clasp and LIBERTY are all plainly visible. Star
centers are partially visible.

REVERSE: Head, neck and leg are worn, but some feathers are visible. Most
details in wings are clear except for outer edges. Talons and arrowheads are
well worn.

FINE
Moderate to heavy even wear. Entire design clear and bold.

OBVERSE: Nearly half the details show in hair, drapery and cap. All letters,
and parts of ear and clasp are visible. Eyelid is flattened. Parts of stars are
worn flat.

REVERSE: Half the feathers are visible in wings. Talons, branch and arrows
are weak but clear. Head is nearly smooth, but eye and some feathers show.

VERY GOOD
Well worn. Design clear but flat and lacking details.

OBVERSE: Entire head outlined with most hair details worn smooth. Eye, ear

QUARTERS—CAPPED BUST 1831–1838

and clasp are barely visible. All letters in LIBERTY are clear. Parts of stars are worn flat.

REVERSE: Eagle is boldly outlined with some feathers showing in wings. Some of the letters are very weak. Head and olive branch are smooth. Talons are separated. Eye is visible.

GOOD
Heavily worn. Design and legend visible but faint in spots.

OBVERSE: Entire design well worn with very little detail remaining. Parts of letters in LIBERTY are worn away. Stars and date are weak but visible and may merge with rim.

REVERSE: Eagle is worn nearly flat, but is completely outlined and shows a few feathers. Tops of some letters are worn nearly smooth and may merge with rim. Eye and talons are only partially visible.

ABOUT GOOD
Outlined design. Parts of date and legend worn smooth.

OBVERSE: Head is outlined with nearly all details worn away. Date readable but very weak. Stars merging into rim.

REVERSE: Entire design partially worn away. Parts of talons are visible. Arrowheads and legend merge with rim.

QUARTERS—LIBERTY SEATED 1838–1891

UNCIRCULATED
Absolutely no trace of wear.

A coin exactly as it was minted, with no trace of wear or injury. May lack full mint luster, and surface may be dull, spotted, or heavily toned.

Check points for signs of abrasion: high points of hair, breast and knees. Neck, claws and tops of wings. Weak spots in the design are usually caused by striking and not wear.

ABOUT UNCIRCULATED
Small trace of wear visible on highest points.

OBVERSE: Traces of wear show on knees, breast, and edge of hairline. Foot is separated from sandal.

REVERSE: Traces of wear show on talons, neck, head, and tips of wings. Half of the mint luster is still present.

EXTREMELY FINE
Very light wear on only the highest points.

OBVERSE: Wear shows on knees, head and shoulder. Gown lightly worn at neckline in spots. LIBERTY is complete and scroll edges are raised.

REVERSE: High points of eagle and arrows are worn, but each detail is clearly defined. Neck feathers and talons are distinct.

Traces of mint luster may still show.

QUARTERS—LIBERTY SEATED 1838–1891

VERY FINE
Light to moderate even wear. All major features are sharp.

OBVERSE: Over half the details still show in the gown. Hair, shoulder, and legs are worn but bold. Neckline is incomplete. Every letter in LIBERTY is visible. Horizontal shield lines are weak at center.

REVERSE: Three-quarters of the feathers are visible. Arrow heads and talons are worn, but some details are visible. Half the details in leaves are clear.

FINE
Moderate to heavy even wear. Entire design clear and bold.

OBVERSE: Some details show in hair, cap, and at the shoulder and breast. All shield lines and letters in LIBERTY are weak but visible. Foot and sandal are separated.

REVERSE: Some details in feathers are visible. Shield border is partially visible on right side. Talons are flat but separated. Letters in legend are worn but clear.

VERY GOOD
Well worn. Design clear but flat and lacking details.

OBVERSE: Entire shield is weak, and most of the gown details are worn smooth. Three letters in LIBERTY are clear. Rim is complete.

QUARTERS—LIBERTY SEATED 1838–1891

REVERSE: Eagle shows only bold outline. Some of the shield is very weak. Leaves are fully outlined. Legend and rim are clear.

GOOD
Heavily worn. Design and legend visible but faint in spots.

OBVERSE: Entire design well worn with very little detail remaining. Date is weak but visible. Shield is worn smooth.

REVERSE: Eagle is worn flat but is completely outlined. Tops of some letters are worn nearly smooth. For coins after 1865, the motto is partially visible.

ABOUT GOOD
Outlined design. Parts of date and legend worn smooth.

OBVERSE: Liberty is outlined with nearly all details worn away. Date readable but very weak. Stars merging into rim.

REVERSE: Entire design partially worn away. Legend merging into rim.

QUARTERS—BARBER 1892–1916

UNCIRCULATED
Absolutely no trace of wear.

A coin exactly as it was minted, with no trace of wear or injury. May lack full mint luster, and surface may be dull, spotted, or heavily toned.

Check points for signs of abrasion: high points of cheek, and hair below LIBERTY. Eagle's head, and tips of tail and wings.

ABOUT UNCIRCULATED
Small trace of wear visible on highest points.

OBVERSE: Traces of wear show on cheek, tips of leaves, and hair below LIBERTY.

REVERSE: Traces of wear show on head, neck, tail, and tips of wings. Half of the mint luster is still present.

EXTREMELY FINE
Very light wear on only the highest points.

OBVERSE: Light wear shows on leaves, cheek, cap and hair above forehead. LIBERTY is sharp and band edges are clear.

REVERSE: High points of head, neck, wings, and tail are lightly worn, but all details are clearly defined. Leaves show trace of wear at edges.

Traces of mint luster may still show.

VERY FINE
Light to moderate even wear. All major features are sharp.

OBVERSE: Over half the details still show in leaves. Hair and ribbon worn but bold. Every letter in LIBERTY is visible.

REVERSE: The shield is worn, but most details are visible. Half the details in feathers are clear. Wings and legs show wear spots. Motto is clear.

FINE
Moderate to heavy even wear. Entire design clear and bold.

OBVERSE: Some details show in hair, cap, and facial features. All letters in LIBERTY are weak but visible. Upper row of leaves is outlined, but bottom row is worn nearly smooth. Rim is full and bold.

REVERSE: Half of the feathers are plainly visible. Wear spots show in center of neck, motto, and arrows. Horizontal shield lines are merged; vertical lines are separated. Letters in legend are worn but clear.

VERY GOOD
Well worn. Design clear but flat and lacking details.

OBVERSE: Entire head weak, and most details in face are worn smooth. Three letters in LIBERTY are clear. Rim is complete.

REVERSE: Eagle shows only a small amount of detail. Arrows and leaves are flat. Most of the shield is very weak. Part of the eye is visible.

QUARTERS—BARBER 1892–1916

GOOD
Heavily worn. Design and legend visible but faint in spots.

OBVERSE: Entire design well worn with very little detail remaining. Legend is weak but visible. LIBERTY is worn away.

REVERSE: Eagle worn flat but is completely outlined. Ribbon worn nearly smooth. Legend weak but visible. Rim worn to tops of letters.

ABOUT GOOD
Outlined design. Parts of date and legend worn smooth.

OBVERSE: Head is outlined with nearly all details worn away. Date readable but partially worn away. Legend merging into rim.

REVERSE: Entire design partially worn away and legend merges with rim.

QUARTERS—LIBERTY STANDING, VARIETY I
1916–1917
UNCIRCULATED
Absolutely no trace of wear.

A coin exactly as it was minted, with no trace of wear or injury. May lack full mint luster, and surface may be dull, spotted, or heavily toned. Head details may be incomplete.

Check points for signs of abrasion: breast, knee, high points of shield, eagle's breast and wings. Coins of this design frequently show weakly struck spots.

ABOUT UNCIRCULATED
Small trace of wear visible on highest points.

OBVERSE: Traces of wear show on head, breast, knee and high points of shield.

REVERSE: Traces of wear show on wing feathers, at center of breast and on tail feathers.

Half of the mint luster is still present.

EXTREMELY FINE
Very light wear on only the highest points.

OBVERSE: Wear shows on head, breast, and right leg above and below knee. At least half the gown line crossing thigh is visible.

QUARTERS—LIBERTY STANDING, VARIETY I
1916–1917

REVERSE: High points of eagle are lightly worn. Central part of edge on right wing is worn flat.

Traces of mint luster may still show.

VERY FINE
Light to moderate even wear. All major features are sharp.

OBVERSE: Right leg is worn nearly flat in central parts. Wear spots show on head, breast, shield and foot. Beads on outer shield are visible, but those next to breast are very weak.

REVERSE: Entire eagle is lightly worn but most major details are visible. Breast, edge of right wing and high parts of left are worn flat.

FINE
Moderate to considerable even wear. Entire design clear and bold.

OBVERSE: Gown details worn nearly smooth across body, but show at sides. Right leg nearly flat and toe is worn. Breast worn but visible.
Date is clear and rim is full. Outer edge of shield is complete.

REVERSE: Eagle is evenly worn. Half of the wing feathers are visible although well worn in spots. The rim is full.

VERY GOOD
Well worn. Design clear but flat and lacking details.

[113]

QUARTERS—LIBERTY STANDING, VARIETY I
1916–1917

GOOD
Heavily worn. Design and legend visible but faint in spots.

OBVERSE: Entire design is weak, and most details in gown are worn smooth. All letters and date are clear. Rim is complete. Drapery across breast is outlined. Bottom right star is worn flat.

REVERSE: About one-third of the feathers are visible, and large feathers at ends of wings are well separated. Eye is visible. Rim is complete.

ABOUT GOOD
Outlined design. Parts of date and legend worn smooth.

OBVERSE: Figure is outlined with nearly all details worn away. Date readable but partially worn away. Legend weak but readable and may merge into rim.

REVERSE: Entire design partially worn away. Some letters merging into rim.

UNCIRCULATED
Absolutely no trace of wear.

A coin exactly as it was minted, with no trace of wear or injury. May lack full mint luster, and surface may be dull, spotted, or heavily toned. One or two small spots may be weakly struck. Head details may be incomplete.

Check points for signs of abrasion: mail covering breast, knee, high points of gown and shield; high points of eagle's breast and wings.

ABOUT UNCIRCULATED
Small trace of wear visible on highest points.

OBVERSE: Traces of wear show on breast, knee and high points of inner shield.

REVERSE: Traces of wear show on edges of wings and at center of breast. All of the tail feathers are visible.

Half of the mint luster is still present.

EXTREMELY FINE
Very light wear on only the highest points.

OBVERSE: Wear shows on breast, and right leg above and below knee. Most of the gown lines are visible. Shield details are bold. Breast is well rounded but has small flat spot.

QUARTERS—LIBERTY STANDING, VARIETY II
1917–1930

REVERSE: High points of eagle are lightly worn. Central part of edge on right wing is well worn.

Traces of mint luster may still show.

VERY FINE
Light to moderate even wear. All major features are sharp.

OBVERSE: Right leg is worn nearly flat in central parts. Wear spots show on head, breast, shield and foot. Beads on outer shield are visible, but those next to body are weak. Inner circle of shield is complete.

REVERSE: Entire eagle is lightly worn but most major details are visible. Breast and edge of right wing are worn flat. Top tail feathers are complete.

FINE
Moderate to considerable even wear. Entire design clear and bold.

OBVERSE: Gown details worn but show clearly across body. Left leg is lightly worn. Right leg nearly flat and toe is worn. Breast worn but some mail is visible. Date may show some weakness at top. Rim is full. Outer edge of shield is complete.

REVERSE: Breast is worn almost smooth. Half of the wing feathers are visible although well worn in spots. The rim is full.

VERY GOOD
Well worn. Design clear but flat and lacking details.

QUARTERS—LIBERTY STANDING, VARIETY II
1917–1930

OBVERSE: Entire design is weak, and most details in gown are worn smooth. All letters and date are clear but tops of numerals may be flat. Rim is complete. Drapery across breast is partially outlined.

REVERSE: About one-third of the feathers are visible, and large feathers at ends of wings are well separated. Eye is visible. Rim is full and all letters are clear.

GOOD
Heavily worn. Design and legend visible but faint in spots.

OBVERSE: Entire design well worn with very little detail remaining. Legend and date are weak but visible. Top of date may be worn flat. Rim is complete.

REVERSE: Eagle worn nearly flat but is completely outlined. Lettering and stars worn but clearly visible. Rim worn to tops of legend.

ABOUT GOOD
Outlined design. Parts of date and legend worn smooth.

OBVERSE: Figure is outlined with nearly all details worn away. Legend visible but half worn away and may merge with rim. Date weak but readable.

REVERSE: Entire design partially worn away. Some letters merging into rim.

QUARTERS—WASHINGTON 1932 TO DATE

UNCIRCULATED
Absolutely no trace of wear.

A coin exactly as it was minted, with no trace of wear or injury. May lack full mint luster, and surface may be dull, spotted, or heavily toned.

Check points for signs of abrasion: high points of cheek, and hair in front and back of ear. Tops of legs, and details in breast feathers.

ABOUT UNCIRCULATED
Small trace of wear visible on highest points.

OBVERSE: Traces of wear show on hair in front and in back of ear.

REVERSE: Traces of wear show on legs and breast feathers.
   Three-quarters of the mint luster is still present.

EXTREMELY FINE
Light wear on most of the highest points.

OBVERSE: Wear shows on high points of hair around ear and at hairline up to crown.

REVERSE: High points of breast, legs, and claws are lightly worn, but all details are clearly defined and partially separated.
   Part of the mint luster is still present.

QUARTERS—WASHINGTON 1932 TO DATE

VERY FINE
Light to moderate even wear. All major features are sharp.

OBVERSE: Three-quarters of the lines still show in hair. Cheek lightly worn but bold. Some hair details around the ear are visible.

REVERSE: Wear shows on breast but a few feathers are visible. Legs are worn smooth. Most details in the wings are clear.

FINE
Moderate to considerable even wear. Entire design clear and bold.

OBVERSE: Details show only at back of hair. Motto is weak but clearly visible. Part of cheek edge is worn away.

REVERSE: Features in breast and legs are worn smooth. Leaves show some detail. Parts of wings are nearly smooth.

VERY GOOD
Well worn. Design clear but flat and lacking details.

OBVERSE: Entire head is weak, and most details in hair are worn smooth. All letters and date are clear. Rim is complete.

REVERSE: About half of the wing feathers are visible. Breast and legs only outlined. Leaves show very little detail. Rim is complete.

QUARTERS—WASHINGTON 1932 TO DATE

GOOD
Heavily worn. Design and legend visible but faint in spots.

OBVERSE: Hair is well worn with very little detail remaining. Half of motto is readable. LIBERTY and date are weak but visible. Rim merges with letters.

REVERSE: Eagle is worn nearly flat but is completely outlined. Leaves, breast and legs are worn smooth. Legend is all visible but merges with rim.

ABOUT GOOD
Outlined design. Parts of date and legend worn smooth.

OBVERSE: Head is outlined with nearly all details worn away. Date readable but worn. Traces of motto are visible. Legend merging into rim.

REVERSE: Entire design partially worn away. Rim merges into legend.

HALF DOLLARS—DRAPED BUST, HERALDIC EAGLE 1801–1807

UNCIRCULATED
Absolutely no trace of wear.

A coin exactly as it was minted, with no trace of wear or injury. May lack full mint luster, and surface may be dull, spotted or heavily toned.

Check points for signs of abrasion: high points of bust, shoulder, and hair above forehead; eagle's head, breast, edges of wings and clouds. Shallow or weak spots in the motto are usually caused by improper striking and not wear.

ABOUT UNCIRCULATED
Small trace of wear visible on highest points.

OBVERSE: Trace of wear shows on hair above forehead. Drapery has trace of wear at shoulder and bustline.

REVERSE: Traces of wear show on breast feathers and clouds.
Half of the mint luster is still present.

EXTREMELY FINE
Very light wear on only the highest points.

OBVERSE: Wear shows on hair from forehead to ear, and lightly on the cheek and bust. Drapery lightly worn at neckline in spots.

REVERSE: High points of clouds and wings are worn, but each detail is clearly defined. Head and breast are slightly worn. Lines in shield are separated.
Traces of mint luster may still show.

HALF DOLLARS—DRAPED BUST, HERALDIC EAGLE 1801–1807

VERY FINE
Light to moderate even wear. All major features are sharp.

OBVERSE: Over half of the details still show in hair. Forehead and bust are worn but bold. Parts of drapery are smooth. Every letter and star is plainly visible.

REVERSE: Head and breast are worn, but some feathers are visible. Some lines in shield are merged together. About three-quarters of details in wings are clear.

FINE
Moderate to considerable even wear. Entire design clear and bold.

OBVERSE: Some details show in hair ends, curls and at left of ear. All letters, date and stars are visible. The eye and eyebrow are clear. Bust is worn with few drapery lines remaining.

REVERSE: Half the feathers are visible in wings. Breast and head are smooth. Letters in legend are worn but clear. Clouds and top of shield show considerable wear.

VERY GOOD
Well worn. Design clear but flat and lacking details.

HALF DOLLARS—DRAPED BUST, HERALDIC EAGLE 1801–1807

OBVERSE: Entire head is weak, and most hair details and drapery are worn smooth. Date and LIBERTY are weak but clear. Parts of the eye and eyebrow are visible. Stars are outlined with some tips worn flat.

REVERSE: Eagle is boldly outlined with only a few details showing in wings. Clouds, head and top of shield are smooth. Some letters in legend are very weak; parts of motto are missing.

GOOD
Heavily worn. Design and legend visible but faint in spots.

OBVERSE: Entire design worn smooth with very little detail remaining. Legend, stars and date are well worn but visible.

REVERSE: Eagle is worn flat and only outlined. Tops of some letters are worn nearly smooth. Only half of the stars are completely outlined. Rim is full.

ABOUT GOOD
Outlined design. Parts of date and legend worn smooth.

OBVERSE: Head is outlined with nearly all details worn away. Date readable but very weak. Stars merging into rim.

REVERSE: Entire design partially worn away. Legend merges with rim.

HALF DOLLARS—CAPPED BUST 1807–1836
UNCIRCULATED
Absolutely no trace of wear.

A coin exactly as it was minted, with no trace of wear or injury. May lack full mint luster, and surface may be dull, spotted, or heavily toned.

Check points for signs of abrasion: drapery at front of bust, cap, shoulder clasp, and hair above eye and at tips of curls. Eagle's claws, head, and edges of wings. Shallow or weak spots in the design are usually caused by improper striking and not wear.

ABOUT UNCIRCULATED
Small trace of wear visible on highest points.

OBVERSE: Traces of wear show on hair above eye and over the ear. Drapery clasp is clear and bold. Cap and drapery around bust show light signs of wear.

REVERSE: Traces of wear show on head, talons, arrow heads, and edges of wings.

Half of the mint luster is still present.

EXTREMELY FINE
Very light wear on only the highest points.

OBVERSE: Wear shows on hair above eye and ear, and lightly on the cap and curls. Drapery lightly worn at neckline in spots. Ear and shoulder clasp are bold. Star details are complete.

HALF DOLLARS—CAPPED BUST 1807-1836

REVERSE: High points of eagle and shield are worn, but each detail is clearly defined. Neck and tail feathers are very lightly worn. Talons, arrows and olive branch show slight wear.

Traces of mint luster may still show.

VERY FINE
Light to moderate even wear. All major features are sharp.

OBVERSE: Over half the details still show in hair. Drapery and lower curls worn but bold. Ear, clasp and curls are worn but all plainly visible. Star centers are very weak.

REVERSE: Head and leg are worn, but some feathers are visible. Most details in wings are clear but edges are flat. Motto is complete. Half of the horizontal shield lines are separated.

FINE
Moderate to considerable even wear. Entire design clear and bold.

OBVERSE: Over half the details show in hair, drapery, and cap. All letters and parts of ear and clasp are visible. Eyelid is flattened. Star centers are worn flat. LIBERTY is complete.

REVERSE: Nearly half the feathers are visible in the wings. Letters in motto are weak but clear. Head is nearly smooth but eye and some feathers show. Parts of shield worn smooth at top.

VERY GOOD
Well worn. Design clear but flat and lacking details.

HALF DOLLARS—CAPPED BUST 1807–1836

OBVERSE: Entire head outlined with half of hair details worn smooth. Eye, ear, and clasp are barely visible. All letters in LIBERTY are readable. Stars are flat.

REVERSE: Eagle is boldly outlined with only a few feathers showing in left wings. Some letters in motto are very weak or partially worn away. Head, top of shield, talons, and olive branch are nearly smooth. Eye is visible.

GOOD
Heavily worn. Design and legend visible but faint in spots.

OBVERSE: Entire design well worn with very little detail remaining. Some letters in LIBERTY are worn away. Stars and date are weak but visible and may merge with rim.

REVERSE: Eagle is worn nearly flat but is completely outlined. Tops of some letters are worn nearly smooth and may merge with rim. Eye and motto are only partially visible.

ABOUT GOOD
Outlined design. Parts of date and legend worn smooth.

OBVERSE: Head is outlined with nearly all details worn away. Date readable but very weak. Stars merging into rim.

REVERSE: Entire design partially worn away.

HALF DOLLARS—CAPPED BUST, REEDED EDGE
1836–1839
UNCIRCULATED
Absolutely no trace of wear.

A coin exactly as it was minted, with no trace of wear or injury. May lack full mint luster, and surface may be dull, spotted, or heavily toned.

Check points for signs of abrasion: drapery at front of bust, shoulder clasp, cap, and hair above eye and at tips of curls. Eagle's claws, arrow heads, and edges of wings.

ABOUT UNCIRCULATED
Small trace of wear visible on highest points.

OBVERSE: Traces of wear show on hair above eye and over the ear. Drapery clasp is clear and bold. Cap and drapery around bust show light signs of wear.

REVERSE: Traces of wear show on talons, arrow heads, and edges of wings. Half of the mint luster is still present.

EXTREMELY FINE
Very light wear on only the highest points.

OBVERSE: Wear shows on hair above eye and ear, and lightly on the cap and curls. Drapery lightly worn at neckline in spots. Ear and shoulder clasp are bold. Star details are complete.

REVERSE: High points of eagle and shield are worn, but each detail is clearly defined. Neck and tail feathers are very lightly worn at center. Talons, arrows and olive branch show slight wear.

Traces of mint luster may still show.

VERY FINE
Light to moderate even wear. All major features are sharp.

OBVERSE: Over half the details still show in hair. Drapery and lower curl worn but bold. Ear, clasp and curls are worn but all plainly visible. Sta centers are weak.

REVERSE: Head and leg are worn, but some feathers are visible. Most detail in wings are clear but edges are flat. Motto is complete. Horizontal shield line are flat but separated.

FINE
Moderate to considerable even wear. Entire design clear and bold.

OBVERSE: Over half the details show in hair, drapery, and cap. All letters and parts of ear and clasp are visible. Eyelid is flattened. Star centers are ver weak. LIBERTY is complete.

REVERSE: Half the feathers are visible in the wings. Talons and arrowhead are flat but clear. Head is nearly smooth but eye and some feathers show Parts of shield worn smooth at top.

VERY GOOD
Well worn. Design clear but flat and lacking details.

HALF DOLLARS—CAPPED BUST, REEDED EDGE
1836–1839

OBVERSE: Entire head outlined with half of all details worn smooth. Eye, ear, and clasp are barely visible. All letters in LIBERTY are readable. Stars are flat.

REVERSE: Eagle is boldly outlined with about half of feathers showing in wings. Head, top of shield, talons, and olive branch are nearly smooth. Eye is visible.

GOOD
Heavily worn. Design and legend visible but faint in spots.

OBVERSE: Entire design well worn with very little detail remaining. At least three letters in LIBERTY are visible. Stars and date are visible but may merge with rim.

REVERSE: Eagle is worn nearly flat but is completely outlined. Tops of some letters are worn nearly smooth and may merge with rim. Eye and shield are only partially visible.

ABOUT GOOD
Outlined design. Parts of date and legend worn smooth.

OBVERSE: Head is outlined with nearly all details worn away. Date readable but very weak. Stars merging into rim.

REVERSE: Entire design partially worn away.

HALF DOLLARS—LIBERTY SEATED 1839–1891
UNCIRCULATED
Absolutely no trace of wear.

A coin exactly as it was minted, with no trace of wear or injury. May lack full mint luster, and surface may be dull, spotted, or heavily toned.

Check points for signs of abrasion: high points of head, breast and knees. Neck, head, beak and tops of wings. Weak spots in the design are usually caused by striking and not wear.

ABOUT UNCIRCULATED
Small trace of wear visible on highest points.

OBVERSE: Traces of wear show on knees, breast, and edge of hairline. Foot is separated from sandal.

REVERSE: Traces of wear show on talons, neck, head, and tips of wings. Half of the mint luster is still present.

EXTREMELY FINE
Very light wear on only the highest points.

OBVERSE: Wear shows on knees, breast, head and shoulder. Drapery lightly worn at neckline in spots. LIBERTY is complete and scroll edges are raised.

REVERSE: High points of eagle and arrows are worn, but each detail is clearly defined. Neck feathers and talons are distinct.

Traces of mint luster may still show.

HALF DOLLARS—LIBERTY SEATED 1839–1891

VERY FINE
Light to moderate even wear. All major features are sharp.

OBVERSE: Over half the details show in the gown. Hair, shoulder, and legs are worn but bold. Every letter in LIBERTY is visible. Horizontal shield lines are weak at center.

REVERSE: Three-quarters of the feathers are visible. Arrowheads and talons are worn, but some details are visible. Half the details in leaves are clear.

FINE
Moderate to considerable even wear. Entire design clear and bold.

OBVERSE: Some details show in hair, cap, and at the shoulder and breast. All shield lines and letters in LIBERTY are weak but visible. Foot and sandal are separated.

REVERSE: Some details in feathers are visible. Shield border is partially visible on right side. Talons are flat but separated. Letters in legend are worn but clear. Letters IN and ST are weak in motto on coins from 1866 through 1891.

VERY GOOD
Well worn. Design clear but flat and lacking details.

OBVERSE: Entire shield is weak but three-quarters outlined. Most gown details are worn smooth. Four letters in LIBERTY are clear. Rim is complete.

REVERSE: Eagle and leaves show only bold outline. Some of shield is very weak. Legend and rim are clear.

GOOD
Heavily worn. Design and legend visible but faint in spots.

OBVERSE: Entire design well worn with very little detail remaining. Date is weak but visible. Shield is worn smooth. Three-quarters of rim is plain.

REVERSE: Eagle is worn flat but is completely outlined. Tops of some letters are worn nearly smooth. For coins after 1865, motto is partially visible.

ABOUT GOOD
Outlined design. Parts of date and legend worn smooth.

OBVERSE: Liberty is outlined with nearly all details worn away. Date readable but very weak. Stars merging into rim.

REVERSE: Entire design partially worn away. Legend merging into rim.

HALF DOLLARS—BARBER 1892-1915

UNCIRCULATED
Absolutely no trace of wear.

A coin exactly as it was minted, with no trace of wear or injury. May lack full mint luster, and surface may be dull, spotted, or heavily toned.

Check points for signs of abrasion: high points of cheek, and hair below LIBERTY. Eagle's head and tips of tail and wings.

ABOUT UNCIRCULATED
Small trace of wear visible on highest points.

OBVERSE: Traces of wear show on cheek, tips of leaves, and hair below LIBERTY.

REVERSE: Traces of wear show on head, neck, tail, and tips of wings.
Half of the mint luster is still present.

EXTREMELY FINE
Very light wear on only the highest points.

OBVERSE: Light wear shows on leaves, cheek, cap and hair above forehead. LIBERTY is sharp and band edges are clear.

REVERSE: High points of head, neck, wings, and tail are lightly worn, but all details are clearly defined. Leaves show trace of wear at edges.
Traces of mint luster may still show.

HALF DOLLARS—BARBER 1892–1915
VERY FINE
Light to moderate even wear. All major features are sharp.

OBVERSE: Over half the details still show in leaves. Hair and ribbon worn but bold. Every letter in LIBERTY is visible. Bottom folds in cap are full.

REVERSE: Shield is worn, but all details are visible. Half the details in feathers are clear. Wings, tail and legs show small wear spots. Motto is clear.

FINE
Moderate to considerable even wear. Entire design clear and bold.

OBVERSE: Some details show in hair, cap, and facial features. All letters in LIBERTY are weak but visible. Upper row of leaves is outlined, but bottom row is worn nearly smooth. Rim is full and bold.

REVERSE: Half the feathers are plainly visible. Wear spots show in center of neck, motto, and arrows. Horizontal shield lines are merged; vertical lines are separated. Letters in legend are worn but clear.

VERY GOOD
Well worn. Design clear but flat and lacking details.

OBVERSE: Entire head weak, and most details in face are heavily worn. Three letters in LIBERTY are clear. Rim is complete.

REVERSE: Eagle shows only a small amount of detail. Arrows and leaves are flat. Most of shield is very weak. Parts of eye and motto visible.

HALF DOLLARS—BARBER 1892–1915

GOOD
Heavily worn. Design and legend visible but faint in spots.

OBVERSE: Entire design well worn with very little detail remaining. Legend and date weak but visible. LIBERTY is worn away.

REVERSE: Eagle worn flat but is completely outlined. Ribbon worn nearly smooth. Legend weak but visible. Rim worn to tops of letters.

ABOUT GOOD
Outlined design. Parts of date and legend worn smooth.

OBVERSE: Head is outlined with nearly all details worn away. Date readable but partially worn away. Legend merging into rim.

REVERSE: Entire design partially worn away and legend merges with rim.

UNCIRCULATED
Absolutely no trace of wear.

A coin exactly as it was minted, with no trace of wear or injury. May lack full mint luster, and surface may be dull, spotted, or heavily toned. A few small spots may be weakly struck.

Check points for signs of abrasion: hair above temple, right arm, left breast; high points of eagle's head, breast, legs and wings. Coins of this design frequently show weakly struck spots, and usually lack full head and hand details.

ABOUT UNCIRCULATED
Small trace of wear visible on highest points.

OBVERSE: Traces of wear show on head, breast, arms and left leg.
REVERSE: Traces of wear show on high points of wings and at center of head. All leg feathers are visible.
Half of the mint luster is still present.

EXTREMELY FINE
Very light wear on only the highest points.

OBVERSE: Wear shows on head, breast, arms and left leg. Nearly all gown lines are visible. Sandal details are complete. Breast and knee are nearly flat.
REVERSE: High points of eagle are lightly worn. Half the breast and leg

HALF DOLLARS—LIBERTY WALKING 1916–1947

feathers are visible. Central part of feathers below neck is well worn.
Traces of mint luster may still show.

VERY FINE
Light to moderate even wear. All major features are sharp.

OBVERSE: Left leg is worn nearly flat. Wear spots show on head, breast, arms and foot. Lines on skirt are visible, but may be weak on coins before 1921. Breast is outlined.

REVERSE: Entire eagle is lightly worn but most major details are visible. Breast, central part of legs, and top edge of right wing are worn flat.

FINE
Moderate to heavy even wear. Entire design clear and bold.

OBVERSE: Gown stripes worn but show clearly, except for coins before 1921 where only half are visible. Right leg is lightly worn. Left leg nearly flat and sandal is worn but visible. Center of body worn but some of the gown is visible. Outer edge of rim is complete.

REVERSE: Breast is worn smooth. Half the wing feathers are visible although well worn in spots. Top two layers of feathers are visible in left wing. Rim is full.

VERY GOOD
Well worn. Design clear but flat and lacking details.

HALF DOLLARS—LIBERTY WALKING 1916–1947

OBVERSE: Entire design is weak; most details in gown are worn smooth except for coins after 1921, where half the stripes must show. All letters and date are clear but top of motto may be weak. Rim is complete. Drapery across body is partially visible.

REVERSE: About one-third of the feathers are visible, and large feathers at ends of wings are well separated. Eye is visible. Rim is full and all letters are clear.

GOOD
Heavily worn. Design and legend visible but faint in spots.

OBVERSE: Entire design well worn with very little detail remaining. Legend and date are weak but visible. Top of date may be worn flat. Rim is flat but nearly complete.

REVERSE: Eagle worn nearly flat but is completely outlined. Lettering and motto worn but clearly visible.

ABOUT GOOD
Outlined design. Parts of date and legend worn smooth.

OBVERSE: Figure is outlined with nearly all details worn away. Legend visible but half worn away. Date weak but readable. Rim merges with lettering.

REVERSE: Entire design partially worn away. Letters merge with rim.

HALF DOLLARS—FRANKLIN 1948–1963
UNCIRCULATED
Absolutely no trace of wear.

A coin exactly as it was minted, with no trace of wear or injury. May lack full mint luster, and surface may be dull, spotted, or heavily toned.

Check points for signs of abrasion: high points of cheek, shoulder, and hair left of ear. Straps around beam, lines and lettering on bell.

ABOUT UNCIRCULATED
Small trace of wear visible on highest points.

OBVERSE: Traces of wear show on cheek and hair on shoulder and left of ear.
REVERSE: Traces of wear show on bell at lettering and along ridges at bottom.

Three-quarters of the mint luster is still present.

EXTREMELY FINE
Very light wear on only the highest points.

OBVERSE: Wear shows on high points of cheek and hair behind ear and at shoulder.
REVERSE: High points of beam straps, and lines along bottom of bell are lightly worn, but details are clearly defined and partially separated. Lettering on bell is worn away at center.

Part of the mint luster is still present.

HALF DOLLARS—FRANKLIN 1948–1963

VERY FINE
Light to moderate even wear. All major features are sharp.

OBVERSE: Three-quarters of the lines still show in hair. Cheek lightly worn but bold. Some hair details around the ear are visible.

REVERSE: Wear shows on beam but most details are visible. Bell is worn but bold. Lines across bottom of bell are flat near crack.

FINE
Moderate to heavy even wear. Entire design clear and bold.

OBVERSE: Hair details show only at back and side of head. Designer's initials weak but clearly visible. Part of cheek is worn flat.

REVERSE: Most of lines at bottom of bell are worn smooth. Parts of straps on beam are nearly smooth. Rim is full.

VERY GOOD
Well worn. Design clear but flat and lacking details.

OBVERSE: Entire head is weak, and most details in hair from temple to ear are worn smooth. All letters and date are bold. Ear and designer's initials are visible. Rim is complete.

REVERSE: Bell is well worn with very little detail remaining. Straps on beam are weak but visible. Rim merges with letters.

HALF DOLLARS—KENNEDY 1964 TO DATE

UNCIRCULATED
Absolutely no trace of wear.

A coin exactly as it was minted, with no trace of wear or injury. Has full mint luster, but surface may be dull, spotted, or heavily toned.

Check points for signs of abrasion: high points of cheek and jawbone, center of neck, hair below part. Bundle of arrows, center tail feather, right wing tip.

ABOUT UNCIRCULATED
Small trace of wear visible on highest points.

OBVERSE: Only a trace of wear shows on highest points of cheek, jawbone and hair below part.

REVERSE: A trace of wear shows on central tail feather.

Nearly all of the mint luster is still present.

EXTREMELY FINE
Very light wear on only the highest points.

OBVERSE: Slight wear shows on cheek, along jawbone and on high points of hair below part. Hair lines are sharp and detailed.

REVERSE: High points of arrows and right wing tip are lightly worn. Central tail feathers are worn but clearly defined and fully separated.

Three-quarters of the mint luster is still present.

VERY FINE
Light to moderate even wear. All major features are sharp.

OBVERSE: Wear spots show on hair below part, and along cheek and jaw. Hair lines are weak but have nearly full visible details.

REVERSE: Wear shows on arrow points but some details are visible. All central tail feathers are plain. Wing tips are lightly worn.

DOLLARS—DRAPED BUST, HERALDIC EAGLE
1798–1804

UNCIRCULATED
Absolutely no trace of wear.

A coin exactly as it was minted, with no trace of wear or injury. May lack full mint luster, and surface may be dull, spotted or heavily toned.

   Check points for signs of abrasion: high points of bust, shoulder and hair above forehead; eagle's head, breast, edges of wings, and clouds. Shallow or weak spots in the motto are usually caused by improper striking and not wear.

ABOUT UNCIRCULATED
Small trace of wear visible on highest points.

OBVERSE: Trace of wear shows on hair above and behind forehead. Drapery has trace of wear at shoulder and bustline.

REVERSE: Traces of wear show on breast feathers and clouds.
   Half of the mint luster is still present.

EXTREMELY FINE
Very light wear on only the highest points.

OBVERSE: Wear shows on hair from forehead to ear, and lightly on the cheek and bust. Drapery lightly worn at neckline in spots.

REVERSE: High points of clouds and wings are worn, but each detail is clearly defined. Head and breast are slightly worn. Lines in shield are separated. Traces of mint luster can be seen.

VERY FINE
Light to moderate even wear. All major features are sharp.

OBVERSE: Over half of the details still show in hair. Forehead and bust are worn but bold. Parts of drapery are smooth. Letters and star centers are plainly visible.

REVERSE: Head and breast are worn, but some feathers are visible. Some lines in shield are merged together. About three-quarters of details in wings are clear. Motto is complete.

FINE
Moderate to heavy even wear. Entire design clear and bold.

OBVERSE: Some details show in hair ends, curls and at left of ear. All letters, date and stars are visible. The eye and ear are clear. Bust is worn with few drapery lines remaining.

REVERSE: Half the feathers are visible in wings. Breast and head are smooth. Letters in legend are worn but clear. Clouds and top of shield show considerable wear.

VERY GOOD
Well worn. Design clear but flat and lacking details.

DOLLARS—DRAPED BUST, HERALDIC EAGLE
1798–1804

OBVERSE: Entire head is weak, and most hair details and drapery are worn smooth. Date and LIBERTY are weak but clear. Parts of the eye and ear are visible. Stars are outlined with some tips worn flat.

REVERSE: Eagle is boldly outlined with only a few details showing in wings. Clouds, head and top of shield are smooth. Some letters in legend are very weak; parts of motto are missing. Rim is full.

GOOD
Heavily worn. Design and legend visible but faint in spots.

OBVERSE: Entire design worn smooth with very little detail remaining. Legend, stars and date are well worn but visible.

REVERSE: Eagle is worn flat and only outlined. Tops of some letters are worn nearly smooth. Only half of the stars are completely outlined. Rim is full.

ABOUT GOOD
Outlined design. Parts of date and legend worn smooth.

OBVERSE: Head is outlined with nearly all details worn away. Date readable but very weak. Stars merging into rim.

REVERSE: Entire design flat and partially worn away. Legend merges with rim.

DOLLARS—LIBERTY SEATED 1840–1873
UNCIRCULATED
Absolutely no trace of wear.

A strictly Uncirculated coin with no trace of wear, but with bag marks and other abrasions. May have a few small rim mars and weakly struck spots. Has full mint luster but may lack brilliance, and surface may be spotted or heavily toned.

For these coins, bag abrasions and scuff marks are considered different from circulation wear. Full mint luster and lack of any wear are necessary to distinguish Uncirculated from About Uncirculated.

Check points for signs of wear: high points of right leg, breast, and hair above eye. Eagle's head, beak, and above eye. Weak spots in the design are usually by striking and not wear.

ABOUT UNCIRCULATED
Small trace of wear visible on highest points.

OBVERSE: Traces of wear show on knees, breast, and edge of hairline. Foot is separated from sandal.

REVERSE: Traces of wear show on talons, neck, head, and tips of wings.
Three-quarters of the mint luster is still present.

EXTREMELY FINE
Very light wear on only the highest points.

OBVERSE: Wear shows on knees, head and shoulder. Drapery lightly worn at neck in spots. LIBERTY is complete and scroll edges are raised.

DOLLARS—LIBERTY SEATED 1840–1873

REVERSE: High points of eagle and arrows are worn, but each detail is clearly defined. Neck feathers and talons are distinct.

Partial mint luster is visible.

VERY FINE
Light to moderate even wear. All major features are sharp.

OBVERSE: Over half the details show in the gown. Hair, shoulder and legs are worn but bold. Every letter in LIBERTY is plainly visible. Horizontal shield lines are weak at center.

REVERSE: Three-quarters of the feathers are visible. **Arrowheads and talons are worn**, but some details are visible. Half the details in leaves are clear. Horizontal lines in shield show wear.

FINE
Moderate to considerable even wear. Entire design clear and bold.

OBVERSE: Some details show in bottom folds of gown, hair, cap, and at shoulder and breast. All shield lines and letters in LIBERTY are weak but visible. Foot and sandal are separated.

REVERSE: Some details in feathers are visible. Most of shield border is visible on right side. Talons are flat but separated. Letters in legend are worn but clear. Horizontal lines in shield heavily worn. For 1866-1873 pieces, IN and ST of motto are weak.

VERY GOOD
Well worn. Design clear but flat and lacking details.

DOLLARS—LIBERTY SEATED 1840–1873

OBVERSE: Entire shield is weak, and most gown details are worn smooth. Four letters in LIBERTY are clear. Rim is complete.

REVERSE: Eagle shows only bold outline. Most horizontal lines in shield are gone. Legend and rim are clear.

GOOD
Heavily worn. Design and legend visible but faint in spots.

OBVERSE: Entire design well worn with very little detail remaining. Date is weak but visible. Shield is worn smooth. Most of rim is visible.

REVERSE: Eagle is worn flat but completely outlined. Tops of some letters are worn nearly smooth. For 1866-1873 pieces, the motto is partially visible.

ABOUT GOOD
Outlined design. Parts of date and legend worn smooth.

OBVERSE: Liberty is outlined with nearly all details worn away. Date readable but very weak. Stars merging into rim.

REVERSE: Entire design partially worn away. Legend merging into rim.

TRADE DOLLARS—1873–1885

UNCIRCULATED
Absolutely no trace of wear.

A strictly Uncirculated coin with no trace of wear, but with bag marks and other abrasions. May have a few small rim mars and weakly struck spots. Has full mint luster but surface may lack brilliance and may be spotted or heavily toned.

For these coins, bag abrasions and scuff marks are considered different from circulation wear. Full mint luster and lack of any wear are necessary to distinguish Uncirculated from About Uncirculated.

Check points for signs of wear: high points of head above ear, left knee and breast. Eagle's head and left wing.

ABOUT UNCIRCULATED
Small trace of wear visible on highest points.

OBVERSE: Traces of wear visible on head above ear, left breast and knee cap. Shoulder and wheat show a trace of wear.

REVERSE: Traces of water show on head and both wings.
Three-quarters of the mint luster is still present.

EXTREMELY FINE
Very light wear on only the highest points.

TRADE DOLLARS—1873–1885

OBVERSE: Wear shows on head and on left leg, foot and breast. Slight wear visible on shoulder and wheat.

REVERSE: Head shows wear but eye is visible and beak clear. Trace of wear visible on leaves at right.

Partial mint luster is visible.

VERY FINE
Light to moderate even wear. All major features are sharp.

OBVERSE: Very little hair detail visible around coronet. Wear shows on knee and leg but knee points are clear. Breasts, shoulder and wheat are worn.

REVERSE: Half of head details and almost three-quarters of wing details are visible. Lettering shows wear, and there are wear spots under E and M of motto.

FINE
Moderate to considerable even wear. Entire design clear and bold.

OBVERSE: Coronet and surrounding detail partially visible. Hair knot shows details. Most stems in wheat are separated. LIBERTY is worn but readable.

REVERSE: Eye, ear and nostril visible on head. Half of wing feathers are visible. Talons show little or no detail. Motto readable but very weak.

VERY GOOD
Well worn. Design clear but flat and lacking details.

TRADE DOLLARS—1873–1885

OBVERSE: Hair at back of lower neck and over left shoulder is visible. Shoulder has a garment line at top. Some wheat stems are separated. Motto is partially visible.

REVERSE: Slight spot visible for eye. One-third of wing feathers shows. Motto is partially readable. Rim is complete.

GOOD
Heavily worn. Design and legend visible but faint in spots.

OBVERSE: Eye is visible as a spot. Nose and mouth are visible. Shoulder is smooth. Very little detail remains in wheat. Motto is gone, and rim merges with stars in spots.

REVERSE: Eagle worn nearly flat but is completely outlined. Motto is gone, and rim merges with letters in spots.

ABOUT GOOD
Outlined design. Parts of date and legend worn smooth.

OBVERSE: Design outlined with nearly all details worn away. Date readable but worn. Rim merging with stars.

REVERSE: Entire design partially worn away. Rim merges into legend.

DOLLARS—MORGAN 1878–1921
UNCIRCULATED
Absolutely no trace of wear.

A strictly Uncirculated coin with no trace of wear, but with bag marks and other abrasions. May have a few small rim mars and weakly struck spots. Has full mint luster but may lack brilliance, and surface may be spotted or heavily toned.

For these coins, bag abrasions and scuff marks are considered different from circulation wear. Full mint luster and lack of any wear are necessary to distinguish Uncirculated from About Uncirculated.

Check points for signs of wear: hair above eye and ear, edges of cotton leaves and blossoms, high upper fold of cap. High points of eagle's breast and tops of legs. Weakly struck spots are common and should not be confused with actual wear.

ABOUT UNCIRCULATED
Small trace of wear visible on highest points.

OBVERSE: Traces of wear show on hair above eye and ear, edges of cotton leaves, and high upper fold of cap. Partial detail visible on tops of cotton blossoms. Luster gone from cheek.

REVERSE: There are traces of wear on breast, tops of legs, wing tips, and talons.

Three-quarters of the mint luster is still present.

EXTREMELY FINE
Very light wear on only the highest points.

DOLLARS—MORGAN 1878-1921

OBVERSE: Wear shows on hair above date, forehead and ear. Lines in hair well detailed. Flat spots visible on edges of cotton leaves. Cheek lightly worn.

REVERSE: Almost all feathers gone from breast. Tops of legs, wing tips and feathers on head show wear. Talons are flat.

Partial mint luster is visible.

VERY FINE
Light to moderate even wear. All major features are sharp.

OBVERSE: Smooth spots visible on hair from forehead to ear. Cotton leaves heavily worn but separated. Wheat grains show wear.

REVERSE: Some leaves on wreath are well worn. Breast is smooth, and only a few feathers show on head. Tips of wings are weak but lines are complete.

FINE
Moderate to heavy even wear. Entire design clear and bold.

OBVERSE: Hairline along face is clearly defined. Lower two cotton leaves smooth but distinct from cap. Some wheat grains merging. Cotton blossoms flat but the two lines in each show clearly.

REVERSE: One-quarter of eagle's right wing and edge of left wing are smooth. Head, neck and breast are flat and merging. Tail feathers slightly worn. Top leaves in wreath show heavy wear.

VERY GOOD
Well worn. Design clear but flat and lacking details.

DOLLARS—MORGAN 1878–1921

OBVERSE: Most details in hair are worn smooth. All letters and date are clear. Cotton blossoms flat, and leaves merging in spots.

REVERSE: Half of eagle's right wing and one-third of left wing are smooth. All leaves in wreath are worn. Rim is complete.

GOOD
Heavily worn. Design and legend visible but faint in spots.

OBVERSE: Hair is well worn with very little detail remaining. Date, letters and design clearly outlined. Rim is full.

REVERSE: Eagle is worn nearly flat but is completely outlined. Design elements smooth but visible. Legend is all visible; rim is full.

ABOUT GOOD
Outlined design. Parts of date and legend worn smooth.

OBVERSE: Head is outlined with nearly all details worn away. Date readable but worn. Legend merging into rim.

REVERSE: Entire design partially worn away. Rim merges into legend.

DOLLARS—PEACE 1921–1935

UNCIRCULATED
Absolutely no trace of wear.

A strictly Uncirculated coin with no trace of wear, but with bag marks and other abrasions. May have a few small rim mars, and may be weakly struck. Has full mint luster but may lack brilliance, and surface may be spotted or heavily toned.

For these coins, bag abrasions and scuff marks are considered different from circulation wear. Full mint luster and lack of any wear are necessary to distinguish Uncirculated from About Uncirculated.

Check points for signs of wear: high points of cheek and hair. High points of feathers on right wing and leg. Weakly struck spots are common and should not be confused with actual wear.

ABOUT UNCIRCULATED
Small trace of wear visible on highest points.

OBVERSE: Traces of wear visible on neck, and hair over ear and above forehead. Cheek shows slight wear.

REVERSE: Traces of wear show on head and high points of feathers on right wing.

Three-quarters of the mint luster is still present.

EXTREMELY FINE
Very light wear on only the highest points.

OBVERSE: Slight flattening visible on high points of hair; most hair strand
clearly separated. Entire face and lower edge of neck lightly worn.

REVERSE: Wear shows on head behind eye and top of neck. Some flat spot
visible on central wing and leg feathers.

Partial mint luster is visible.

VERY FINE
Light to moderate even wear. All major features are sharp.

OBVERSE: Very little hair detail visible around face. Wear shows on upper
wave of hair. Hair above ear worn but some single strands are clear.

REVERSE: Detail on right wing worn but the three horizontal lines of feather
layers show. Flattening visible on leg feathers and neck. Motto and talon
lightly worn.

FINE
Moderate to heavy even wear. Entire design clear and bold.

OBVERSE: All hair around face is smooth. Slight wear shows on hair at back
of neck and on bun. Rays show a trace of wear.

REVERSE: All feathers on right leg are worn away. Lower third of neck
feathers visible. Only the lowest horizontal line of feather layers will show
Parts of PEACE and E PLURIBUS weak but readable.

VERY GOOD
Well worn. Design clear but flat and lacking details.

DOLLARS—EISENHOWER 1971–1978

OBVERSE: Slight wear shows on cheek, along jawbone and on high points at edge of bust. Hair lines are sharp and detailed.

REVERSE: High points of head, legs and wing ridges are lightly worn. Central feathers are all clearly defined.

Three-quarters of the mint luster is still present.

VERY FINE
Light to moderate even wear. All major features are sharp.

OBVERSE: Wear spots show on hair below part, and along cheek and jaw. Hair lines are weak but have nearly full visible details. Slight wear shows at center of neck and along edge of bust.

REVERSE: Wear shows on head, and feathers in wings and legs but all details are visible. All central tail feathers are plain. Wing and leg ridges are lightly worn.

DOLLARS—ANTHONY 1979–1981

UNCIRCULATED
Absolutely no trace of wear.

A strictly Uncirculated coin with no trace of wear, but with bag marks and other abrasions. May have a few small rim mars and weakly struck spots. Has full mint luster but may lack brilliance. Lack of any wear and full mint luster are necessary to distinguish Uncirculated from About Uncirculated.

Check points for signs of wear: cheekbone, hair in center of head, and collar button. Head, high points of ridges and feathers in wings and legs.

ABOUT UNCIRCULATED
Small trace of wear visible on highest points.

OBVERSE: Traces of wear show on cheekbone, hair and collar button.

REVERSE: Traces of wear show on head, and high points of ridges and feathers in wings and legs.

Three-quarters of the mint luster is still present.

GOLD DOLLARS—TYPE I 1849–1854
UNCIRCULATED
Absolutely no trace of wear.

A coin exactly as it was minted, with no trace of wear or injury. May lack full mint luster and brilliance.

Check points for signs of abrasion: hair near coronet; tips of leaves.

ABOUT UNCIRCULATED
Small trace of wear visible on highest points.

OBVERSE: There is a trace of wear on hairlines near coronet, and below the ear.

REVERSE: Trace of wear visible on tips of leaves.
Half of the mint luster is still present.

EXTREMELY FINE
Very light wear on only the highest points.

OBVERSE: Slight wear shows on highest wave of hair, hairline, and below ear. All major details are sharp. Beads at top of coronet are well defined.

REVERSE: Leaves show visible wear at tips but central details are clearly defined.

Traces of mint luster will show.

GOLD DOLLARS—TYPE I 1849–1854

VERY FINE
Light to moderate even wear. All major features are sharp.

OBVERSE: Beads at top of coronet are partially separated. LIBERTY is complete. Hair around face and neck noticeably worn but well outlined. Some star centers show details.

REVERSE: There is light even wear on legend and date. Only traces of leaf ribs are visible. Bow knot is flat on high point.

FINE
Moderate to heavy even wear. Entire design clear and bold.

OBVERSE: LIBERTY is complete but weak. Ear lobe is visible. Hairlines, and beads on coronet, are worn smooth. Stars are clearly outlined, but centers are flat.

REVERSE: Legend within wreath is worn and weak in spots. Leaves and wreath are well outlined. Rim is full and edge beveled.

VERY GOOD
Well worn. Design clear but flat and lacking details.

OBVERSE: Only the outline of hair is visible. Four letters in LIBERTY are clear.

GOLD DOLLARS—TYPE I 1849–1854

REVERSE: Only the outline of leaves is visible. Legend and numeral are worn and very weak.

GOOD
Heavily worn. Design and legend visible but faint in spots.

OBVERSE: Head is outlined with nearly all details worn away. Stars are weak. Full rim shows.

REVERSE: Date and legend well worn but readable. Leaves are outlined. Full rim shows.

GOLD DOLLARS—TYPE II 1854–1856

UNCIRCULATED
Absolutely no trace of wear.

A coin exactly as it was minted, with no trace of wear or injury. May lack full mint luster and brilliance. Check points for signs of abrasion: hair over Liberty's eye; bow knot.

ABOUT UNCIRCULATED
Small trace of wear visible on highest points.

OBVERSE: There is a trace of wear on hair over eye, at curl below ear, and at top of feathers.

REVERSE: Trace of wear visible on tips of leaves and bow knot.
   Half of the mint luster is still present.

EXTREMELY FINE
Very light wear on only the highest points.

OBVERSE: There is slight wear on highest wave of hair, on hairline, below ear, on top of feathers, and on cheek. All major details are sharp.

REVERSE: Slight wear shows on tips of leaves, bow knot, wreath, legend and date.
   Traces of mint luster will show.

GOLD DOLLARS—TYPE III 1856–1889

UNCIRCULATED
Absolutely no trace of wear.

A coin exactly as it was minted, with no trace of wear or injury. May lack full mint luster and brilliance.

Check points for signs of abrasion: hairline over Liberty's eye; bow knot.

ABOUT UNCIRCULATED
Small trace of wear visible on highest points.

OBVERSE: There is a trace of wear at hairline and at top of feathers.

REVERSE: Trace of wear visible on tips of leaves and on bow knot.
  Half of the mint luster is still present.

EXTREMELY FINE
Very light wear on only the highest points.

OBVERSE: Slight wear shows at hairline, on hair near ear, tops of feathers, and on cheek. All major details are sharp.

REVERSE: Slight wear shows on tips of leaves, bow knot, wreath, legend and date.
  Traces of mint luster will show.

GOLD DOLLARS—TYPE III 1856–1889
VERY FINE
Light to moderate even wear. All major features are sharp.

OBVERSE: Hair, feathers, and curl tips are outlined with only slight detail. LIBERTY worn but visible.

REVERSE: Bow knot well worn. Slight detail visible in leaves. Some indentation remains on cotton bolls.

FINE
Moderate to heavy even wear. Entire design clear and bold.

OBVERSE: Hair and some feathers smooth. Ear lobe visible. Part of LIBERTY worn almost smooth.

REVERSE: Bow knot, leaves and cotton bolls outlined only, with no details visible.

QUARTER EAGLES—CLASSIC HEAD 1834–1839
UNCIRCULATED
Absolutely no trace of wear.

A coin exactly as it was minted, with no trace of wear or injury. May lack full mint luster and brilliance.

Check points for signs of abrasion: hair and cheek; wings.

ABOUT UNCIRCULATED
Small trace of wear visible on highest points.

OBVERSE: There is a trace of wear on hair above forehead, at top of head, above eye and ear.

REVERSE: Trace of wear visible on head and top edges of wings.
Half of the mint luster is still present.

EXTREMELY FINE
Very light wear on only the highest points.

OBVERSE: Light wear shows on high points of hair. Slight wear visible on cheek. Stars sharp with details visible.

REVERSE: Slight wear shows on top edges of wings, feathers, neck and head. Shield well defined.
Traces of mint luster will show.

QUARTER EAGLES—CLASSIC HEAD 1834-1839

VERY FINE
Light to moderate even wear. All major features are sharp.

OBVERSE: Hair outlined with very little detail. Only a few stars show any details. LIBERTY worn but clear.

REVERSE: Half of wing and neck feathers are visible. Some details show in shield.

FINE
Moderate to heavy even wear. Entire design clear and bold.

OBVERSE: Hair and cheek smooth. Stars outlined with no details visible. LIBERTY worn but visible.

REVERSE: Some of wing and neck feathers visible. Eagle's head is smooth. Shield shows little detail.

QUARTER EAGLES—CORONET HEAD 1840–1907

UNCIRCULATED
Absolutely no trace of wear.

A coin exactly as it was minted, with no trace of wear or injury. May lack full mint luster and brilliance.

Check points for signs of abrasion: tip of coronet, hair; wings, claws.

ABOUT UNCIRCULATED
Small trace of wear visible on highest points.

OBVERSE: There is a trace of wear on coronet and on hair above ear, eye, and forehead.

REVERSE: Trace of wear visible on wing tips, below eye and on claw.
Half of the mint luster is still present.

EXTREMELY FINE
Very light wear on only the highest points.

OBVERSE: Light wear shows on coronet, hair above ear and eye, on forelocks, and on cheek. All major details sharp.

REVERSE: Light wear shows on edges and tips of wings, on neck, below eye, on feathers and claws. Shield well defined.
Traces of mint luster will show.

QUARTER EAGLES—CORONET HEAD 1840–1907

VERY FINE
Light to moderate even wear. All major features are sharp.

OBVERSE: Hair outlined with very little detail. Only a few stars show any details. LIBERTY clear but not bold.

REVERSE: Half of wing feathers visible. Half of lines in shield are clear.

FINE
Moderate to heavy even wear. Entire design clear and bold.

OBVERSE: Hair and cheek smooth. Stars outlined with no visible details. LIBERTY worn but visible.

REVERSE: Wings show very little detail. Head and one claw outlined only, with no details visible. Neck almost smooth. Most of shield lines merge.

QUARTER EAGLES—INDIAN HEAD 1908–1929

UNCIRCULATED
Absolutely no trace of wear.

A coin exactly as it was minted, with no trace of wear or injury. May lack full mint luster and brilliance.

Check points for signs of abrasion: cheekbone, headdress, headband feathers; shoulder of eagle's left wing.

ABOUT UNCIRCULATED
Small trace of wear visible on highest points.

OBVERSE: There is a trace of wear on cheekbone and headdress.

REVERSE: Trace of wear visible on shoulder of wing, head and breast.
Half of the mint luster is still present.

EXTREMELY FINE
Very light wear on only the highest points.

OBVERSE: Light wear shows on cheekbone, jaw, and headband. Slight wear visible on feathers of headdress. Stars sharp.

REVERSE: Light wear shows on wing, head, neck and breast. Leg has full feather detail.
Traces of mint luster will show.

QUARTER EAGLES—INDIAN HEAD 1908–1929

VERY FINE
Light to moderate even wear. All major features are sharp.

OBVERSE: Cheekbone worn about halfway. Small feathers clear, but large feathers show a little detail. Hair cord knot is distinct. Headband shows some detail.

REVERSE: Little detail shows on breast and leg feathers. Top of wing and neck worn. Second layer of wing feathers shows.

FINE
Moderate to heavy even wear. Entire design clear and bold.

OBVERSE: Cheekbone worn; all feathers worn with very little detail visible. Stars outlined, with no details visible. Hair cord knot is worn but visible.

REVERSE: Wing worn, with only partial feathers at bottom visible. All lettering worn but visible.

THREE-DOLLAR GOLD PIECES—1854–1889

UNCIRCULATED
Absolutely no trace of wear.

A coin exactly as it was minted, with no trace of wear or injury. May lack full mint luster and brilliance.

Check points for signs of abrasion: above eye, tops of feathers; bow knot, leaves.

ABOUT UNCIRCULATED
Small trace of wear visible on highest points.

OBVERSE: There is a trace of wear on top curves of feathers and on high parts of hair.

REVERSE: Trace of wear visible on bow knot and tips of leaves.
Half of the mint luster is still present.

EXTREMELY FINE
Very light wear on only the highest points.

OBVERSE: Light wear shows on tops of feathers. Hair shows wear but all details visible.

REVERSE: Light wear visible on bow knot, leaves, and wreath.
Traces of mint luster will show.

THREE-DOLLAR GOLD PIECES—1854–1889

VERY FINE
Light to moderate even wear. All major features are sharp.

OBVERSE: Curled feathers and hair near curls show slight details. Beads and LIBERTY clear.

REVERSE: Bow knot well worn. Slight detail visible in leaves. Some indentation remains on cotton bolls.

FINE
Moderate to heavy even wear. Entire design clear and bold.

OBVERSE: Curled feathers smooth. Hair smooth with very little detail showing. Beads partially visible. LIBERTY weak but readable.

REVERSE: Bow knot, leaves and cotton bolls outlined only, with no details visible.

HALF EAGLES—CLASSIC HEAD 1834–1838

UNCIRCULATED
Absolutely no trace of wear.

A coin exactly as it was minted, with no trace of wear or injury. Has full mint luster but may lack brilliance. Surface may be lightly marred by minor bag marks and abrasions.

Check points for signs of wear: hair; wings.

ABOUT UNCIRCULATED
Small trace of wear visible on highest points.

OBVERSE: There is a trace of wear on high point of hair, above eye and ear.

REVERSE: Trace of wear on wings and head.

Half of the mint luster is still present.

EXTREMELY FINE
Light wear on only the highest points.

OBVERSE: Hair well defined with light wear on high points. Slight wear shows on cheek. Stars sharp with all details visible.

REVERSE: Light wear visible on wings, feathers, neck and head. Shield shows very light wear but is well defined.

Traces of mint luster will show.

HALF EAGLES—CLASSIC HEAD 1834–1838

VERY FINE
Light to moderate even wear. All major features are sharp.

OBVERSE: Hair outlined with some detail showing. Most detail in stars visible. Ear lobe worn. LIBERTY shows wear but is complete.

REVERSE: Half of wing and neck feathers visible.

FINE
Moderate to heavy even wear. Entire design clear and bold.

OBVERSE: Headband edges worn. Hair outlined with very little detail. Half the detail in stars visible. Ear outlined only. LIBERTY complete but some letters weak.

REVERSE: Some of wing and neck feathers are visible. Head almost smooth but shows slight detail. Some details in shield visible.

VERY GOOD
Well worn. Design clear but flat and lacking details.

OBVERSE: Cap outlined at top; hair and cheek smooth. Most of LIBERTY visible. Hardly any detail shows in stars.

REVERSE: Eagle shows very little detail.

HALF EAGLES—CORONET HEAD 1839–1908

UNCIRCULATED
Absolutely no trace of wear.

A coin exactly as it was minted, with no trace of wear or injury. Has full mint luster but may lack brilliance. Surface may be lightly marred by minor bag marks and abrasions.

Check points for signs of wear: hair, coronet; wings.

ABOUT UNCIRCULATED
Small trace of wear visible on highest points.

OBVERSE: There is a trace of wear on coronet, above ear and eye.

REVERSE: Trace of wear visible on wing tips, below eye and on claw.
Half of the mint luster is still present.

EXTREMELY FINE
Light wear on only the highest points.

OBVERSE: Light wear shows on coronet, on hair above ear and eye, on the forelock, on top of head and on cheek. All major details are sharp.

REVERSE: Light wear visible on edges and tips of wings, on neck, below eye, on feathers and claws. Shield is well defined.
Traces of mint luster will show.

HALF EAGLES—CORONET HEAD 1839–1908

VERY FINE
Light to moderate even wear. All major features are sharp.

OBVERSE: Hair worn but major details visible. Top line of coronet broken. Some stars show partial detail. LIBERTY clear but not bold.

REVERSE: Half of wing feathers are visible. Half of lines in shield are clear.

FINE
Moderate to heavy even wear. Entire design clear and bold.

OBVERSE: Hair and cheekbone smooth. Top line of coronet worn. LIBERTY worn but visible.

REVERSE: Wings show very little detail. Head and one claw outlined only, with no details visible. Neck almost smooth. Most of shield lines merge. (For the 1866 through 1908 group, the motto is worn but readable.)

HALF EAGLES—INDIAN HEAD 1908–1929

UNCIRCULATED
Absolutely no trace of wear.

A coin exactly as it was minted, with no trace of wear or injury. Has full mint luster but may lack brilliance. Surface may be lightly marred by minor bag marks and abrasions.

Check points for signs of wear: cheekbone, headdress, headband feathers; shoulder of eagle's left wing.

ABOUT UNCIRCULATED
Small trace of wear visible on highest points.

OBVERSE: There is a trace of wear on cheekbone and headdress.

REVERSE: Trace of wear visible on shoulder of wing, head and breast.
Half of the mint luster is still present.

EXTREMELY FINE
Light wear on only the highest points.

OBVERSE: Light wear shows on cheekbone, jaw and headband. Slight wear visible on feathers of headdress. Stars are sharp.

REVERSE: Light wear shows on wing, head, neck and breast. Leg has full feather detail.

Traces of mint luster will show.

HALF EAGLES—INDIAN HEAD 1908–1929

VERY FINE
Light to moderate even wear. All major features are sharp.

OBVERSE: Cheekbone worn about half-way. Headdress feathers show some details. Hair cord knot is distinct. Headband shows only a little detail.

REVERSE: Little detail shows on breast and leg feathers. Top of wing and neck worn. Second layer of wing feathers shows.

FINE
Moderate to heavy even wear. Entire design clear and bold.

OBVERSE: Cheekbone worn; all feathers worn with very little detail visible. Stars outlined, with no details visible. Hair cord knot is worn but visible.

REVERSE: Wing worn, with only partial feathers at bottom visible. All lettering worn but visible.

EAGLES—CORONET HEAD 1838–1907

UNCIRCULATED
Absolutely no trace of wear.

A coin exactly as it was minted, with no trace of wear or injury. Has full mint luster but may lack brilliance. Surface may be lightly marred by minor bag marks and abrasions.

Check points for signs of wear: hair, coronet; wings.

ABOUT UNCIRCULATED
Small trace of wear visible on highest points.

OBVERSE: There is a trace of wear on hair at ear and above eye, and on coronet.

REVERSE: Trace of wear visible on wing tips, below eye and on claw.
Half of the mint luster is still present.

EXTREMELY FINE
Light wear on only the highest points.

OBVERSE: Light wear shows on coronet, hair, cheek and stars. All major details sharp.

REVERSE: Light wear visible on wings, head, neck and claws. Shield is well defined.
Traces of mint luster will show.

EAGLES—CORONET HEAD 1838–1907

VERY FINE
Light to moderate even wear. All major features are sharp.

OBVERSE: Hair worn but major details visible. Break on top line of coronet extends over at least three letters in LIBERTY. Cheek well worn. Stars worn but show most details. LIBERTY clear but shows wear.

REVERSE: About half of wing feathers are visible. Very little detail shows in head.

FINE
Moderate to heavy even wear. Entire design clear and bold.

OBVERSE: Hair and cheekbone smooth. Top line of coronet worn. Some details show in stars. LIBERTY worn but visible.

REVERSE: Wings show very little detail. Head and one claw outlined only, with no details visible. Neck is almost smooth. Most of shield lines merge. (In the 1866 through 1907 group, the motto is worn but readable.)

EAGLES—INDIAN HEAD 1907–1933

UNCIRCULATED
Absolutely no trace of wear.

A coin exactly as it was minted, with no trace of wear or injury. Has full mint luster but may lack brilliance. Surface may be lightly marred by minor bag marks and abrasions.

Check points for signs of wear: above eye, cheek; wing.

ABOUT UNCIRCULATED
Small trace of wear visible on highest points.

OBVERSE: There is a trace of wear on hair above eye and on forehead.

REVERSE: Trace of wear visible on wing.
Half of the mint luster is still present.

EXTREMELY FINE
Light wear on only the highest points.

OBVERSE: Light wear shows on hair, cheekbone, and feathers.

REVERSE: Light wear visible on wing and head.
Traces of mint luster will show.

EAGLES—INDIAN HEAD 1907–1933

VERY FINE
Light to moderate even wear. All major features are sharp.

OBVERSE: About half the hair detail is visible. Moderate wear shows on cheekbone. Some feathers do not touch headband.

REVERSE: There is moderate wear on left wing which shows only about one-quarter detail. Head almost smooth. All lettering bold.

FINE
Moderate to heavy even wear. Entire design clear and bold.

OBVERSE: Hair smooth with no details; cheekbone almost smooth. No feathers touch headband but most feather details visible.

REVERSE: Left wing top and head are worn smooth. Lettering worn but visible.

DOUBLE EAGLES—LIBERTY HEAD 1850–1907

UNCIRCULATED
Absolutely no trace of wear.

A coin exactly as it was minted, with no trace of wear or injury. Has full mint luster but may lack brilliance. Surface is usually lightly marred by minor bag marks and abrasions.

Check points for sign of wear: hair, coronet; eagle's neck and wing, top of shield.

ABOUT UNCIRCULATED
Small trace of wear visible on highest points.

OBVERSE: There is a trace of wear on hair at top and over eye, and on coronet.

REVERSE: Trace of wear visible on wing tips, neck and at top of shield.
  Half of the mint luster is still present.

EXTREMELY FINE
Light wear on only the highest points.

OBVERSE: Light wear shows on hair, coronet prongs and cheek.

REVERSE: Light wear visible on wings, head, neck, horizontal shield lines and tail.

  Traces of mint luster will show.

[187]

DOUBLE EAGLES—LIBERTY HEAD 1850–1907

VERY FINE
Light to moderate even wear. All major features are sharp.

OBVERSE: Less than half the hair detail above coronet visible. About half the coronet prongs are considerably worn. Stars are flat but show most details. LIBERTY shows wear but is very clear.

REVERSE: Some wing details visible. Shield shows very little detail at top. Tail is worn with very little detail.

FINE
Moderate to heavy even wear. Entire design clear and bold.

OBVERSE: All hairlines well worn with very little detail visible. About one-quarter of details within coronet visible. Stars show little detail. LIBERTY readable.

REVERSE: Wings show very little detail. Head and neck smooth. Eye visible. Tail and top of shield smooth.

DOUBLE EAGLES—SAINT-GAUDENS 1907–1932

UNCIRCULATED
Absolutely no trace of wear.

A coin exactly as it was minted, with no trace of wear or injury. Has full mint luster but may lack brilliance. Surface is usually lightly marred by minor bag marks and abrasions.

Check points for signs of wear: forehead, breast, knee, nose; eagle's wings and breast.

ABOUT UNCIRCULATED
Small trace of wear visible on highest points.

OBVERSE: There is a trace of wear on nose, breast and knee.

REVERSE: Trace of wear visible on wings.
Half of the mint luster is still present.

EXTREMELY FINE
Light wear on only the highest points.

OBVERSE: Light wear shows on forehead, nose, breast, knee and just below left knee. Drapery lines on chest visible.

REVERSE: Light wear visible on wings and breast but all feathers bold.
Traces of mint luster will show.

DOUBLES EAGLES—SAINT-GAUDENS 1907–1932

VERY FINE
Light to moderate even wear. All major features are sharp.

OBVERSE: Forehead moderately worn. Contours of breast worn. Only a few garment lines on chest are visible. Entire right leg shows moderate wear.

REVERSE: Half of feathers are visible in wings and breast.

FINE
Moderate to heavy even wear. Entire design clear and bold.

OBVERSE: Forehead and garment smooth; breasts flat. Both legs worn with right bottom missing.

REVERSE: Less than half the wing details are visible. Only a little breast detail is visible.

CONTENTS

CONTENTS—Continued